CW01498214

THE UNHEARD STORIES

THE UNHEARD STORIES

CELEBRATING TEN YEARS OF THE
SI LEEDS LITERARY PRIZE

EDITED BY SAIMA MIR

PEEPAL TREE

First published in Great Britain in 2023
Peepal Tree Press Ltd
17 King's Avenue
Leeds LS6 1QS
England

ISBN13: 9781845235802

Supported using public funding by
ARTS COUNCIL
ENGLAND

CONTENTS

SAIMA MIR

INTRODUCTION

The contributors to this book tell stories that resonate with each other and with mine. They are of the experience of meeting common barriers and the need for extraordinary efforts to overcome them. They are also very individual accounts of women with very different things they want to say. It is both the commonality of the experience of being ignored by the mainstream publishing industry and the immense diversity within the labels "Black", "Asian" and "Women" revealed in the essays in this collection that make both what they have to say and the SI Leeds Literary Prize so necessary and important.

My father came to the UK in the late 1960s and mother followed in the 1970s. They left behind them their networks of friends, colleagues and contacts. That is a common experience for migrants. You begin again in a place where you don't have those things, networks that many within the publishing industry take for granted. When I first began dreaming of becoming a writer, I spent many years sitting at my desk, looking out onto the promised land of publishing wondering what you had to do to achieve entry.

Despite having worked as a journalist for almost twenty years, having won awards, and written articles that went viral on *The Guardian* website, I encountered much rejection. I couldn't find a publisher ready to buy my novel. I believed that if I just worked harder, tried a little more, committed more fervently to my craft, a path would appear. Eventually it did; it wasn't paved with gold, but by then I was willing to accept anything. Having a book published is one thing; having it promoted is another. I'd seen younger counterparts race past me, hitting the finish line at breakneck speed in comparison to my tortoise pace. It was depressing and made me doubt my abilities. I considered quitting on countless occasions.

Much has been written about the glass ceiling, the social barrier that stops women reaching the highest echelons of society, but for women of colour, the glass walls that encase us are so smooth and seemingly transparent that during the business of living we forget they are there. Between us and publication stands this great glass edifice, on whose walls we bang our heads as we attempt to pass through. The reminder comes every time we try to enter rooms where women who look like us have not been welcome before, and when we pull up chairs to sit at tables where previously we have been declined service.

Things changed for me in 2019, after Bernardine Evaristo, who is one of the patrons of the SI Leeds Literary Prize, won the Booker Prize with *Girl, Woman, Other* and became a *Sunday Times* bestseller, holding the coveted position for five weeks. All of the sudden, booksellers realised that women of colour were bankable writers, and placed orders for our work with publishers. In my case, Waterstones, ordered 2500 blood-splattered (it is a crime novel) copies of my debut novel, and chose it as their book of the month. Their support was critical to the success of *The Khan*. Since then, booksellers such as Waterstones and newspapers such as the *Sunday Times* and *The Times* have supported other talented women of colour including award-winning crime writer, Kia Abdullah.

Despite these wins, we have yet to reach the promised land. The structures that kept us out as marginal to networks that are predominantly white and middle class are still in place. We are in a strange middle phase where all of us are stumbling towards each other, our white counterparts and our Black and Asian sisters, hitting this pane of glass between us, the fingerprints of women who have tried and failed for countless years still visible.

Even when commissioning editors want to buy our manuscripts, they stumble at the hurdle of acquisitions and advances offered, because the structures in place use historical evidence to set the level of purchase and justify low figures. Agents offering something new operate in territory without precedents, so the numbers to back the book up as good business (with the right level of promotion) simply don't exist.

It is here that the SI Leeds Literary Prize finds itself. By championing Black and Asian women writers and giving us a platform, by supporting our work, and signposting and signal-boosting, the prize arms writers with the tools they need to follow their dreams.

Over time, I have found my allies outside of the words that have historically been used to define me, and box me in as a Muslim woman of Pakistani heritage. The intersection on which I stand is also brown, female, northern, mother, mother-of-sons, writer, living in SW London. This increases the ways I have available to connect, and find common ground with others. It is only by coming together across these intersections that we will smash the glass prison in which we find ourselves. It has been harder than it should be to get beyond the labels we are given, but we have to because outside of them lies our power.

Fibre by fibre, our individual capacities spin into yarns to twist into strong ropes of diversity, which individual members of society can use pull themselves up out of the enclosing glass walls. Our stories will remain unheard until we unite to shatter the walls themselves, and it's more effective and safer to knock down glass walls from outside than within them.

None of this is easy. I'm aware of the challenges we face in coming to a consensus about life which acknowledges its actual multiplicity and variety, but with respect and faith we can bring about real, sustainable change.

One of the ways we do this is by speaking our truths and telling the stories of our experiences. If we don't do this, those who aren't of the same shade or gender, or those who don't share the vista from which we view the world, can never understand what it feels like to be us. The only way to do it is to cup our hands, fill them with our stories and offer them as a cool drink to each other.

During the years I struggled to be published, questions from people and the fact that I wasn't being paid for my work drove me to ask myself if I really was a writer. I am the same person now, with the same abilities, as I was then. The stamp of approval brought with it the realisation that my work as a writer is still the same (it is still a solitary occupation depending on your imagination and hard work), but it needs the assistance of a team who edits, who markets and promotes and is prepared to invest in building a novelist's profile.

It is trite but true that if you put words on paper or a screen, you are a writer. But craft takes time, and in a world where we need to feed our children and pay our bills we need the remuneration that comes with the stamp of approval. Financial freedom allows the creative muscle time to relax and do its thing, it gives writers permission to take the vital thinking time that crafting a story requires; it helps to make our work better.

The SI Leeds Literary Prize has been and is a vital weapon in the armoury, in the continuing battles towards ending racism, and misogyny, including in the publishing world that rejected us over and over again. It gives us a safe space to gather, to find reassurance and comfort in our work and our value as writers. It has supported us to have the confidence to know we must no longer accept the crumbs offered, because we are better than that, because our stories are powerful, life-changing, and important.

Within this anthology you will find stories told by women who write. These are the stories that they want to tell, and they don't need permission to tell them. We share them with you as a gift. They are a record of the work that we have done. Our mark that we were here, that we wrote and that our work is of value.

VALERIE SAUNDERS

THE SI LEEDS LITERARY PRIZE:
HOW IT ALL BEGAN

Looking back, it's quite difficult now to remember when the SI Leeds club was not associated with the SI Leeds Literary Prize. And it has grown beyond our initial expectations into something beyond our imaginings. So why did we start it?

The context is of course the SI Leeds club, and I need to provide a bit of background and history. Soroptimist International (SI) is a worldwide women's organisation set up more than a hundred years ago. Through its network of national clubs and five international federations, its aim is to work collectively to transform the lives of women and girls. SI strives to do this by as many means as possible, from the macro (large international projects and advocacy) to the very local. Individual clubs such as SI Leeds have a part to play in larger initiatives, but they also seek to make a difference through their own projects. These are developed depending both upon perceived need and the interests, skills and contacts of their members.

The SI Leeds club is one of the older clubs in the UK; it has been going since 1930. In its earlier days in particular, the club provided a crucial professional and support network for the rising numbers of well-educated professional women seeking to make their way in an exceedingly male-dominated world.

The majority of these women were single. Also, throughout its life, the Leeds club has always looked for innovative and, sometimes, groundbreaking projects that will have a positive impact on the lives of women, and meet the core aims of Soroptimism.

During 2010, having concluded work on a number of ongoing activities, the Leeds club was looking for a new project. One of our members, Gail Bolland, (who has also contributed to this anthology), spotted a project that was being run by one of the French clubs, SI Grenoble. Grenoble was offering an annual prize for fiction in the French language to women resident in France, for whom French was not their first language. On the basis that imitation is the sincerest form of flattery, Gail thought that the Leeds club might consider doing something similar.

Although not unsupportive in principle, initially the Leeds club had a number of completely justified doubts, including:

-   How on earth do you run a literary prize?
-   What should its focus be?
-   How much would it cost?

If this idea were to be pursued, we clearly needed partners, and a meeting was arranged with Rachel Feldberg, the then-Director of Ilkley Literature Festival. She was enthusiastic from the start about a new literary prize and with her we drafted an outline proposal agreed by her Festival Board. This clarified that the prize would be national, that it would be for new, unpublished fiction (a novel or a short story collection), that it would be biennial (we hoped!) and that it would be an award for UK-based Black and Asian women, a much under-represented group in UK published literature.

From the club's perspective as well, this target group of

women was also important – as with many other SI clubs in the UK, in demographic terms the membership of the Leeds club did not reflect the makeup of the city's female population. It was hoped that the Prize would help to spread the net of potential membership more widely.

The critical next step was to find a partner from the world of publishing. The ideal choice was Peepal Tree Press, a wholly independent Leeds-based company publishing Caribbean and Black British authors. PTP was also enthusiastic. Right from the start, the intention was to offer the winner, and, indeed, the shortlisted writers, professional development support, and initially this would be through Peepal Tree's Inscribe writer development programme. The possibility of publication of the winning entry if the work was deemed to be of sufficient quality was also offered.

The club had agreed a budget (inevitably inadequate, as it turned out) for the first round of the prize. A steering group was established, with members representing the three core partners. Provision had been made to appoint a project manager, on a very part-time basis, as none of the club members had the time or expertise actually to get the prize underway. Fiona Goh was appointed in May 2011. As a freelance arts consultant with experience of working with literature organisations and festivals, she came with ideal credentials, and she had also worked with Ilkley Literature Festival. Throughout its lifetime, Fiona has been a linchpin of the prize and its development. Now the Prize Director, she has also contributed to this anthology.

Given the target group of women writers whom we were hoping to attract, and as part of the momentum for launching the Prize, we then set about enlisting as many high profile patrons as we could. It became apparent that Peepal Tree Press and Ilkley Festival between them had a dazzling array of contacts. It was heart-warming that many of them were happy to be included as soon as they were approached. The full list of our patrons can be found on our website – early recruits included Margaret Busby, Bidisha, Bernardine Evaristo, Bonnie Greer and Yasmin Alibhai-Brown, who has also contributed to this anthology. Our patrons have supported us in many ways, and lent vital visibility to the prize over the past ten years.

So the first prize was launched at Ilkley Literature Festival in October 2011. Despite early concerns that there would only be a handful of entries, there were actually sixty-five, all submitted to Peepal Tree, who took on the task of sifting them and then sending entries on to the judges. It had been agreed that 1st, 2nd and 3rd place prizes would be awarded by the judges. In addition, there was to be a special 'SI Readers' Choice' award. This involved as many SI readers as wanted to be included – they would each read the six shortlisted manuscripts and vote for them in order of preference. The highest score would win. In practice, this involved Peepal Tree in a mammoth task, including printing copies for those who did not have computer access.

The first award event, held at the 2012 Ilkley Festival, was an extremely happy one – chaired by Margaret Busby, as the first head judge, and including a memorable conversation she had with her invited guest and prize patron, Bonnie Greer.

From its modest beginnings, the prize has grown and thrived. The process is now slicker, with bespoke software being used for all the steps in the submitting and judging process. Social media have been an increasingly important factor in publicising the prize and its successes. The funding, although always a concern for each prize round, has grown over time, with substantial grants from Arts Council England and generous sponsorship from The Opportunity Centre, based in Bradford. SI Leeds continues to contribute the prize money for the three placed authors, and for the winner of the SI Readers' Choice. Our partnerships continue to grow, so that our six shortlisted writers have a number of development opportunities which are at least as important to them as the prize itself.

The core partnership, of SI Leeds with Ilkley Literature Festival and Peepal Tree Press, has stood the test of time, and has been fundamental to the prize's success. We managed to adapt and survive during the Covid lockdown, with key events being shifted online. Despite continuing funding anxieties each time – in this regard we are no different from any other arts initiative – we always travel hopefully to the next prize round. We are very proud that the prize has been at the very least a stepping stone in the writing careers of so many talented women. Long may it continue.

FIONA GOH

WHAT'S NEXT?

When the SI Leeds Literary Prize was launched in 2011, Margaret Busby held up a copy of her pioneering anthology, *Daughters of Africa*, published some 20 years previously, and asked what had changed. The short answer was: not enough. That anthology had been heralded by *The Washington Post* Book World as "A magnificent starting place for any reader interested in becoming part of the collective enterprise of discovering and uncovering the silent, forgotten, and underrated voices of Black women." One could be forgiven for asking where that starting place might eventually lead, given the dearth of diversity on our bookshelves. The latest *Bookseller* survey makes depressing reading in this context – the relative increase in interest in Black writers following the murder of George Floyd in 2020 doesn't seem to have made a lasting, sustainable change in the industry, and the figures for 2023 are lower in terms of numbers of Black writers in the top 1000 highest earners for the year, their earnings and market share.

Margaret Busby was the first Chair of judges for the Prize in its inaugural edition in 2012 and remains a Prize Patron and Ambassador. She was the youngest female publisher in UK history, and the country's first Black woman publisher when she co-founded Allison & Busby in 1967. She is one of a series of remarkable women who have made the prize possible, and have shaped and encouraged its development. This award was the brainchild of Members of Soroptimist International of Leeds, notably Gail Bolland and Val Saunders – both featured elsewhere in this volume – and Val remains a hugely important driving force behind the prize, providing both a clear-sighted steer and professional support in moving us in the right direction. We wouldn't have been able to make the journey today without the founding partnership of Ilkley Literature Festival, now Word up North, and Peepal Tree Press, who continue to be with us every step of the way, even in the 'knitting with fog' years when we were first establishing the award.

Indeed, I believe that one of the real strengths of the prize has come out of the way that we made that journey together, 10 years ago, by effectively making it up as we went along. As the first literary award for unpublished fiction by Black and Asian women writers, we knew we were forging a new path anyway, so it gave us freedom to shape the prize in exactly the way we wanted. The partnerships we've made over these 10 years have enabled the prize to grow and shift, creating a unique ecosystem of support and camaraderie amongst our alumnae, and we've been blessed to have such generous, loyal support from our partners. The 2022 cohort of prize longlisted and shortlisted writers have received the broadest package of prize benefits yet, including not only cash awards and serious consideration for publication by Peepal Tree Press, but also a range of development opportunities through Arvon, The Literary Consultancy, New Writing North and Mslexia, as well

as mentoring from fellow prize alumnae. There's something about the chemistry of these prize plus benefits,
including the opportunities for our shortlist to appear at
literary events together, which has cemented a lovely bond
between our writers, some of whom continue to meet
regularly many years after the prize awards.

On this level, then, the prize acts as a network and a
support group for an industry that can feel arcane, difficult
to access and positively unwelcoming at times. Sharmaine
Lovegrove, another former prize judge, agrees that changes
in the post-George Floyd landscape don't reflect a lasting
difference in the sector: "My perspective as managing
director of Dialogue, as well as Co-organiser of the Black
Writers' Guild and a member of the Black Agents & Editors
Group, is that it was really bittersweet to watch so many
authors' work go for such high advances as I feared for the
long-term strategy in this short-term investment. I want
authors to be paid well for their work, as a business
decision, not a political one, but I knew the work behind
the scenes to engage audiences wasn't being done in the
majority of cases. Three years after the murder of George
Floyd and after #BLM has been taken down from many
publishing Twitter bios, most of those books are not
reaching the stratospheres required from the high advances. This means a renewed lack of confidence and back
to a 'we have one' attitude at many imprints across London
publishing."

The growth of a prize family as a much-needed support
network has been a joy to watch over the last decade. My
own sense of pride when a prize alumna gets an agent, is
shortlisted for a prize or has her prize manuscript published, is immense but this is also reflected across the

network. It's been fantastic to witness that first-hand support of fellow prize alumna attending each other's book launches and offering practical help and advice in career development. And although our bookshelves continue to be far too monochrome, there are rainbow flashes of brilliance. Bernardine Evaristo was one of the Prize's earliest Patrons, and has been alongside us in the journey over this first 10 years, both at our events and to uphold our writers. Her Booker success in 2019 felt like a real game changing moment but what will it take for us to reach the point where the SI Leeds Literary Prize is no longer relevant, and no longer needed?

Our unique focus on unpublished fiction is part of the key to answering this question. We've had such a brilliant array of entries during the first decade of the prize, from speculative fiction to short stories, crime to historical, sci-fi to romance. As in this anthology, the prize's central importance is for authors to be given the freedom to write what they truly want to write, rather than what they think publishers will want to publish. We will continue to be a space that enables women writers of colour until the time is reached when the publishing industry moves past 'one and done', and narrow pre-conceptions of what our authors might create.

There have been several moments during the last ten years when we may have doubted the feasibility of the journey we were on – when we have had funding knock-backs, or lower numbers of prize submissions – and then we were hit by a post-Brexit or post-Trump xenophobic battering against everything that we stand for, and we have had to simply redouble our efforts.

So, what's next for the prize and what does that tell us

about what's next for the industry? We've been on quite a journey during the last ten years, and learned lots about what we need in our toolbox in order to keep us moving forward into the next decade:

- **More resilience than we thought we would have needed**: resilience is an over-used word in our sector, where tenacity and sheer determination often significantly outweigh cash, but its importance is not any the less for that. Support from our incredible family of writers really helps when things are tough, and there's no better package to arrive on your doorstep than a new publication from a prize alumna – it's just a joy, and builds an additional layer of resilience against the next challenge.

- **Nimble feet**: we moved very quickly during the pandemic, with our pace of learning just about keeping up with the extremely fast pace of change. Being forced to adapt in a crisis has given us all confidence about our ability to stay on our toes as the world continues to change at huge speed.

- **Relentless partnership building:** we've continued both to grow existing partnerships and build new ones, and each new relationship has set off a chain reaction of development that we couldn't have anticipated before it began. As we plan for the next ten years of the prize's development, having brilliant partners is the solid foundations that will enable us to reach high in our ambitions for our writers and for the award.

- **To want more**: we need to keep knocking on the door of the industry until it doesn't just open a crack but actually changes shape in order to let everyone in. When we get a little, we need to keep asking for more. I often think about Andy Dufresne in *The Shawshank Redemption* asking for support towards a prison library; he redoubled his efforts after a positive – if paltry – response from the state to his repeated requests: "It only took 6 years. From now on, I'll write two letters a week instead of one."

So, what has changed since *Daughters of Africa* (1992), or indeed *New Daughters of Africa* (2019)? Not enough. We go on. Please join us: our voices will be stronger if we shout together.

YASMIN ALIBHAI BROWN

WHAT I WANTED. WHAT I STILL WANT.

I've lived a long time. There have been exhilarating periods, happy times and periods of intense vexation and weariness. But still I write, push out boundaries.

Growing up in the Empire, being forced to migrate to the UK, settling here in the inclement seventies, and through the ensuing decades, I have had to slowly, insistently, make my voice heard, my face seen. Even now, after winning a host of journalistic awards, I grapple with various controllers in the newspaper, broadcast and book industries, often feeling abjectly dependent and occasionally, triumphant. I go on because I must. After I have passed on, my ghost may well bother and harangue commissioning editors.

I wrote my first journalistic piece when I was 37. All writers say writing is hard and, also a compulsion. If you are black and Asian, you have added incumbrances. Most gatekeepers are uninformed about our multifaceted, complex nation[1] and think of the minorities as marginal people, living in the unknowable, impenetrable peripheries. Our talents and contributions, do get recognised, but half-heartedly or patronisingly, or due to a shift in the social environment,[2] mostly because untapped markets can deliver profits. The dynamic advertising industry understands the monetary rewards of inclusive capitalism. Too many other creative sectors remain relatively sluggish and smug.[3]

At many London gatherings of the cultured, well-connected and well-read, I maybe see a handful of black and Asian guests. There are exceptions. The Women's Prize, Author's Society and Royal Society of Literature events reflect the rainbow nation. But most arty parties remain closed to 'outsiders'.

If you are brown or black, you get over-effusive greetings and compliments and quite a lot of faux pas. They say: 'I love your columns in the *Guardian*'. I correct them: 'Er I don't write for the *Guardian*' and think, but don't say: 'The Guardian treats me like I'm a nobody, and now keeps me off its pages for reasons I don't know. So, actually, I buy the paper, but can't abide the editors, some of whom are black and brown.'

Then there is this: 'My, you *are* controversial!' Or 'provocative!' or 'brave!' Do they think I choose to rile people? Or do people get riled when they see/hear my name? I write honestly, without fear or favour. As do, say, the *Guardian*'s Marina Hyde, or *Sunday Telegraph*'s Janet Daley. Do they get asked these questions in that arch way, with lifted eyebrows? It feels like a code to me, a code saying, you don't know your place. Which, truth to tell, I don't.

Too many high-achieving individuals of colour have these experiences. Acceptance and admiration are always conditional. Dependent on good behaviour. Stuff that.

Today's Britain is undeniably more open than in the bad old days. Change has been slow but transformative. Maybe that's why many middle-class, liberal custodians, are becoming chary of cultural expansiveness. I'll give you one such example. In May 2023, at the Design Museum in London, previously a white bastion, 'The Offbeat Sari', was curated by Priya Khanchandani, a Royal College of Art alumnus. Exciting, imaginative young designers are re-forming the ancient garment. Coco Khan, in the *Guardian*, Billi Bhatia, in *Vogue* and I, in the *I* newspaper – both brown – raved about the show. Pale, male critics didn't get it all. Some whined that traditional saris they had seen in India were being dishonoured. This is the context. Too many of us are still not seen or heard on our terms.

Back to my writing and its trajectory. I never trained to be a journalist. One day I sat down and typed a column on an Amstrad, haltingly, slowly. At a party the previous evening no one had pronounced my name properly. I mean how hard is Yasmin? Yas (s as in sun) min? Why Yazmin, or Jasmine? The column was about that and also absent histories. Many guests expressed sympathy for Asians expelled from Uganda by the 'terrible' Idi Amin. That was nice of them. But when I moved the conversation to British, American, and Israeli support for the tyrant, shutters came down, and the shoulders turned cold. As we know, British history is always glorious.

That first column was emotional, authentic, and strong. I showed it to Aidan White, a journalist at the *Guardian*. He sent it to a section editor who published it. (That newspaper gave me my first break. For that I remain grateful.) After that I successfully pitched to various publications, and slowly built up a portfolio. The early work was all about race, ethnicity, faith, and minority concerns. Yes, it was tokenism, but tokenism is a step through the door. I knew I could explore those issues with insight and knowledge because I was an insider. My white colleagues, of course believed that they, being 'objective' and 'professional', knew it all. That ignorance/arrogance still prevails across the media. Just think of the bosses who commissioned TV series and book, *Rick Stein's India* (2013) and Michael Portillo's 20-part *Asian Railway Journeys* (2020, BBC). Then think of their colonial thinking.

Six months after that first ever column, I got a job at *New Society* magazine. This was in 1987. Then came the explosive, lifechanging Rushdie affair. Back in 1988, thousands of British Muslims, deeply offended by the *Satanic Verses* began peaceful protests. They were scorned and slated by white liberals. The collective fury was unbearable. I'd always believed that faith was a private matter. But as the atmosphere became toxic and all British Muslims were demonised, I, at the time, probably the only Muslim working in the national press, came out as a Muslim. This was before the fatwa. I abhor book-banning or burning and fatwas. But citizens should have the right to protest non-violently against books or films, art, etc. If religion isn't sacred, nothing else should be.

On BBC Radio4, I reminded listeners that an entire print-run of *Massacre*, a book disparaging clerics by the French cartoonist Sine, was burned in 1967, by Allen Lane, the publisher, after some people in the establishment said they were offended by the publication and in 1976, Prime Minister Callaghan, the Archbishop of Canterbury and the Queen intervened to prevent director Jens Jorgen Thorsen from making a film in Britain on the sex life of Jesus. Furthermore, I added, libel laws and editorial decisions surely attest to the fact that there is no absolute right to free speech. That interview led to exclusion from the airwaves, fellow journalists picking fights and even some walkouts at dinner parties. As I say, there's no such thing as free speech.

I was at the *New Statesman* at the time. Its editor deliberately censored the views of Muslims who were upset by the novel. I left, left a job I never thought someone like me would ever have. I needed the income. Just before I departed, the Islamophobic editor spiked an article I had written for the magazine about racism in GB. I sold it to *The Guardian*. My boss exploded with anger. The *Guardian* commissioning editor paid me a pittance. When I objected, he told me superciliously that I should be more 'grateful'. All this was before the Ayatollah's appalling fatwa.

Years later, when I had made a name for myself and married Mr Brown, an old New Statesman colleague, an Englishman – drunkenly – said this to me at a party: 'You've done well. Of course, you couldn't have done it without that 'Brown' in your surname. That was a smart gambit'. My response? 'Thanks. Just imagine where I'd be if I'd married a Mr White!'

Was I treated with true respect by my white peers? Some. Many, most, were disdainful because I wasn't writing on Westminster games (BORING) or wars or business.

Book publishers are a little more enlightened than decision-makers in my sector. Even so, I have found myself boxed in, labelled and wilfully misunderstood. My ideas and I make them nervous, edgy. When trying to get a publisher for *The Settler's Cookbook*, a memoir peppered with memorable dishes, my then agent took me to meet cookbook editors – all absurdly young. No, they said, 'no market for Indian cookbooks'. Eventually Portobello commissioned it. It still sells across the globe. Exotic England came next. It explored England's complicated relationship with eastern nations – exploitative, supremacist and yet amorous. I suggested that English painters in Egypt and India were not all Orientalists, that some of their paintings were affectionate and elegiac. And described the Indo-Saracenic architectural influence on St Paul's Cathedral. The certainties of anti-Orientalists and traditional Englanders were unsettled. They didn't like that at all.

'Unsettling' is what I think I am. It's what I have always done. As I write this, I am trying to get a book published. The same old biases and incomprehension are surfacing. I will get there. Always do. Feeling sore, tired and bursting with creative energy. Wish me well.

(Endnotes)
1. See my book, *Who Do We Think We Are?* (Allen Lane, 2000).
2. #blacklivesmatter and #MeToo, for example, triggered big changes.
3. By that I mean the gatekeepers believe they have done more than enough on diversity, which to them is a project with an end, not a process that is without end.

KAVITA BHANOT

LITERATURE AND LIFE

It is a truth universally acknowledged today, that reading literature is good for us.

This, like the original version of the quote in Jane Austen's *Pride and Prejudice*, is an exaggeration of course. For example, my grandmother, who passed away a few years ago aged 85, did not think that reading literature was good for anyone, in particular women. There was an occasion when my grandmother, impatient for my attention, grabbed the book I was reading and flung it across the room. She would tell me stories about the 'madman' in her childhood village in Punjab, who read too much, who asked too many questions, who the children threw stones at. Soon after my marriage, my grandmother told my mother-in-law to keep an eye on me, making sure I didn't waste time reading and writing. Years before, she had told me about my grandfather's cousin's wife, who was apparently 'addicted' to reading stories, leading her to neglect her husband, children, home and responsibilities. While she lived in the UK, her children were apparently sent away from her, to their grandparents in India. Her husband left her and remarried, she started drinking too much; her body was found, days after her death, in the flat she lived in alone. All this was, according to my grandmother, because of her reading 'addiction'.

This was a fabricated story, I discovered later as I enquired about this tragic female relative. Whether or not she 'read too much', whatever she read or if she read at all – the truth is that she was treated badly and eventually abandoned by her husband, apparently because she was 'dark skinned'. My grandmother's version of this story was a product of her internalised patriarchal mindset, which not only condemned this woman and defended her male cousin-in-law, but also used the story as a 'lesson' to try to convince me to prioritise marriage and 'women's work' and discourage me from 'too much' reading and writing.

It was my grandmother's characteristic lack of empathy for the oppressed that bothered me when she told me this story, rather than her attitude towards reading. There is a tendency in popular culture and literature, to construct enemies of literature – whether it is Matilda's parents, Jeanette Winterson's mother, Islamists in *Reading Lolita in Tehran* or the school authorities in *Dead Poet's Society*. The implication, in this popular trope, is that their mistrust or ambivalence or dislike of literature makes these figures questionable – this is a cause or manifestation of their lack of empathy, ethics and imagination. Reading, and writing, in these constructions, become almost heroic acts of resistance.

I have a desire neither to romanticise my grandmother nor reading and writing.

It would be absurd to construct my grandmother as a threatening figure; she was the epitome of a vulnerable immigrant woman. Like all the girls and women in her family, she spent most of the first twenty years of her life confined in a small family home in Mandi, her village in Punjab. This was due to patriarchy, but also caste supremacy, that expressed itself through concealing, controlling and 'protecting' brahmin women (internalising both patriarchy and Brahminical supremacy, my grandmother did not see herself as confined or controlled – only protected.) After marriage, when my grandfather got a job with the Delhi Milk Scheme, she lived for some years in Delhi. Aged thirty, she moved with her husband and three children to Britain via a 'voucher scheme' that brought many Punjabis to the UK in the sixties, to fill a labour shortage in British factories and foundries. She worked in factories for many years and would tell me about the complaints white women made about her and other South Asian women; for keeping to themselves, for speaking their own language, for eating their food, for not using English toilets 'properly'. She gathered a minimal grasp of spoken English in the few years she spent serving customers in the family shop in South London. Otherwise, she spoke Punjabi and, thanks to a few years of schooling in her local village school (enough to write letters home after marriage) she read and wrote basic Hindi. She was widowed at 42 when her husband, my grandfather, was hit by a truck (three days after my dad arrived in the UK from India to marry my mother) while crossing the road.

However, my grandmother was also far from the saintly, mythical grandmother figure, keeper of magical ancestral knowledge and wisdom I see depicted in decolonial literature these days. Along with upholding internalised patriarchy, she was Brahminical and Casteist, Islamophobic, Anti-Black; in other words, she was a bundle of vulnerabilities and supremacies (perhaps vulnerabilities lead us to draw all the more on our supremacies, in a distorted attempt to grasp for self-esteem.)

It didn't occur to me to connect my grandmother's prejudices to her antipathy for literature or vice versa. It was always clear to me that my grandmother was not prejudiced because she didn't read. Nor would reading have made her less prejudiced. Whether or not she read, she would have been the same person.

Coming from a context where there often isn't time, skills or inclination to read books, where people are not judged, dismissed or demonised for *not* reading, and knowing that a vast world exists *outside* of, far away from books, I have never been disposed to make judgements about those who don't read. I saw my grandmother's attitude to literature as reflecting a widespread suspicion across the world towards literature as an unknown entity – seeing it as frivolous and unimportant compared to the practical work that needed to be done. This is understandable for those (women, working classes, immigrants) whose worth is measured through practical work/labour, indeed whose survival depends on this. I could empathise with her ambivalence towards literature, having also often questioned the importance of reading and writing over in-person interactions, conversations, oppression and suffering. Reading and writing has mostly always been an activity for the privileged few.

Although I was not inclined to judge my grandmother's attitude to literature, the truth is that the reading woman in my grandmother's story did intrigue me. I struggle to think of women relatives, particularly of that generation, who loved to read. Perhaps I thought of this woman as an ally across the generations, someone I could relate to. Looking back, the search for reader-mentors or allies has been a thread throughout my life, perhaps because of my own lifelong obsession with literature, perhaps because I felt 'different' growing up. (Although it is important to highlight that this sense of 'difference' did not come from feeling like an oppressed figure – as we often see in representations of young readers from marginalised, working class, immigrant backgrounds – but an internalised feeling of superiority.)

It's not that I'm the only person in my family who loved reading. My siblings have always read fiction. My mother would tell me that, as a teenager, a recent migrant to the UK learning English, she went through a phase of reading constantly. But my obsession was something else.

I grew up amidst a large busy family, a home full of joy and depression, laughter and tears, music and silence, cooking and cleaning, people coming and going, sometimes staying for weeks or months. I had friends at school, but this was where the friendships remained: it was a time before mobile phones and social media and after-school socialising was not encouraged. I didn't mind. My friendships at school didn't feel as if they went deep, infiltrating my inner life. I was shy, I didn't share much of myself, my life, my thoughts and feelings; school felt alien, a place to be endured. My 'real' life was at home, and it was mostly entangled in books and art. When I wasn't taking care of my younger sister and cousins, when I wasn't ironing or cooking or listening to music or painting and drawing, I lay on the upper berth of the bunk bed I shared with my two sisters, reading. Whether visiting family and family friends, attending satsangs and kirtans, throughout the trips I would be lost in a book.

From the age of seven, for the next ten years, until I was seventeen, I read 2-3 books (mostly novels) a week, sometimes one or two a day. Once or twice a week I would go to the library to top up my supply. I read about the holocaust, including *Anne Frank's Diary*, about slavery, including *Roots,* about apartheid in South Africa, about the Napoleanic wars in Russia, I read the Brontes and Jane Austen, Maya Angelou and Buchi Emecheta, Daphne Du Maurier and George Eliot, D.H. Lawrence and Charles Dickens.

It felt as if my immersion in these books and worlds that were different from mine, 'revealed' (to echo a cliché) other worlds, places and times; they broadened my horizons, giving me empathy for others. They helped me through difficult periods – I was not as deeply impacted by the turmoil in the home and racism outside, as my three siblings, perhaps because, through the escapism that these books offered, I was mostly elsewhere. I have recently been diagnosed with ADHD, perhaps my 'addiction' to reading during this period was a manifestation of the 'zoning out' that Gabor Maté writes about: a child's response to stress in the immediate environment. At the same time, reading seemed to centre me, helped me to focus, was almost a form of meditation. I would say that in those years I lived more in literature than in the world.

But this is not an essay about my reading life, my life in books. It's easy to slip into romanticism about both books and childhood, and I certainly carry a deep affection for this period of my life which I associate with my absorbing relationship with books, with the worlds and people contained between those book covers. As my relationship with the world grew more complex and entangled, I was never quite able to recreate the same investment and trust in literature. A niggling critical voice in my head grew louder and louder.

As I started writing myself, as I sought out reader-writer allies across the world, those who had been similarly formed by books (with the assumption, so often purveyed in popular culture, that they are the good people, that this is my tribe), as I started to question the structures and hierarchies of the world, comparing what I saw around me and its representation in books, including in my own writing, I started to question the mythmaking around literature.

While fiction can challenge dominant perspectives, it also often reflects and builds on white, upper-class and caste, patriarchal ideologies and perspectives, including those in the literature that precedes it. Writing fiction myself has revealed to me, over the years, the layers, assumptions, supremacies and walls in my own perspective and writing. Meanwhile, I found readers and writers to be no better, morally, ethically, politically, than those who don't read and write. Sometimes, because of their privilege combined with their conviction (superiority even) that that are the good ones, they are even worse.

Looking back now, I try to understand the ways in which the literature I read as a child influenced me. At the time, there was nobody to share or discuss the journey with, so it was, in many ways, a one-way journey of absorption and influence. Perhaps I simply did not know enough about the world, about the specific contexts I was reading about, to understand that these books weren't a mirror to a place or a people or a time. A book represents the perspective and experience of an individual writer who is also formed by wider influences: by school, media, culture, other literature. At times, writers might challenge some dominant assumptions, but there will always be people and oppressions that the writer does not see, having internalised the eyes of the world. I trusted the literature I was reading instead of understanding that there are always more layers to any place and people than those presented in books – there are those who are mocked and demonised, those who are relegated to the margins, those who are erased, not seen. Books represent a version or slice of life, not life itself.

Do I believe then, that literature has no worth? No. The truth is that my life is entangled in literature – reading, writing, editing, translating, researching, discussing and teaching it. It is central to my life. But I don't believe that I need to elevate, mystify, or idealise literature to justify this focus. In fact, through every aspect of my work with literature, I seek to connect it with the world and people, to normalise irreverence and critical engagement.

LYNNE E BLACKWOOD

DIFFERENT

We're all born different. Whether by birth or acquired through life, our differences always amaze me. I've seen people feel uncomfortable when standing out from the general environment: a European in an Asian or African cultural environment or country and the inverse situation: someone with disabilities attempting to attend events when hampered by a wheelchair or other mobility aids – and many other examples of how our diversity can make us stand out in societies, whether in a good or bad way. Coming from a Scottish and Parsi Indian mixed heritage and culture, where three-generational family reunions are dotted with various combinations of genes, I revel in our differences. Dark skin, blue eyes with white-blonde hair; auburn with freckles, or a black hair and dark skin Indian look – we have it all, including the cultural heritage of warmth and kindness towards the elderly and weaker members of our wide family circle.

But after the past decade of political and social shifts in British society, it's become harder to be different, hasn't it? So, where did my journey begin? On a Friday 13th, I came into this world with my head stuck in a toilet bowl, cord strangling my neck, blue and not breathing. I now take this as a premonition of things to come. A superstitiously unlucky day, but I survived, just as I have survived until now, though maybe that's just a personal interpretation since I've never felt unlucky in my life – only tossed about in occasional storms when unexpected events push me further across the ocean of experiences. My father is no longer alive to tell me what he thought and felt about the birth of his first-born. The only scant details available were provided by my mother many years later and judging by her unwillingness to expand further, I can only presume this wasn't an occasion of joy.

Here I am, a twenty-month-old toddler sitting in the garden, one chubby hand clutching a chunk of crusty bread, the other held out to feed small birds clustered at bare feet. A butterfly settles on one brown arm, another on the mass of white-blond curls surrounding my tanned face. Mother looks on from the kitchen window, dishwashing cloth suspended in mid-motion at the disturbing scene of her strange child who's also being greeted excitedly by the notoriously ferocious dog of the street, an Alsatian who bites and growls at everyone except me. When I pass by, he rolls over, tail wagging, whimpering with delight. I attract anything that flies, crawls or walks. I'm 'strange', different and horribly precocious, already marked as an outsider in life, an eternal looker-on from the sidelines of society.

My tall and fair Scottish mother probably believed I was a changeling baby switched by fairies, as she stared at the darked-skinned newborn endowed with black hair growing vertically like a coconut tuft. She desperately tried to brush my hair flat but in vain, eventually tying a ribbon around the obstinate growth and having to accept the reality of the very distinctive creature in the pram. Once, drinking too much wine during a rare visit caused her to explain how I'd frightened her right from birth. My ability to attract animals, insects, birds, and other unmentionable things scared the wits out of her, especially since I was also precocious in everything. I already talked like a six-year-old at the age of two, stringing together sentences that contained constant refrains of 'why', 'how', 'what' etc. Mother didn't know what to do with me, especially when I was two and came holding a crayon and a piece of paper covered in letters copied from books and badgered her, articulating clearly that I wanted to learn to read and write.

My father was posted to Singapore when I was three and a half and I have a vivid recollection of my parents taking me to the Army school and arguing with the teacher about accepting me at the tender age of four. The sceptical teacher handed me a first reading book, then the second, followed by the series, to conclude with a reluctant acceptance. I returned from tropical Singapore two years later with a reading age of ten and an unacceptable shade of brown, to rural Wiltshire and to a 1950's Army base, still an unforgiving colonial outpost. My father was widely known to be Euro-Indian and although as a child I was not consciously aware of being different, with hindsight I realise I was treated as an exotic oddity with the additional problem of precociousness. *"Too smart for you own good"*, excluded from skipping with girls in the playground because I was always *"teacher's pet"* and *"too brown"*, always far ahead of other schoolchildren, always alone, looking on longingly from the outside, preferring to play Mahjong with my father and his Gurkha soldiers who regularly visited our house. My father experienced the same 'differences' as an immigrant after Partition and fortunately taught me how to ignore jibes and name calling.

Family context and upbringing are important for children to weather lifelong discriminations when they are considered different. Educational establishments dispensing safe environments and promoting understanding of our diversity are essential from an early age. Given the complex family structures of today, schools should offer an alternative for children who lack these. You can't learn empathy, but kindness and tolerance can be taught. I was lucky to thrive in that kind of environment.

Although I began life with noticeable differences, in addition to having inherited my father's Parsi Indian genes, this wasn't the greatest influence on why I always felt an outsider. I can now acknowledge with a sigh of relief and an *"ah, that's why"*, what I didn't know then – synaesthesia. A condition which jumbles all the senses together and heightens them, creating acute observation skills for small details and exacerbated empathy and sensitivity verging on what could be called a sixth sense with increased perception for anyone and anything. Synaesthesia offers the capacity to become excellent multitaskers with an innate capacity to grasp the bigger picture and anticipate strategically. Everything is captured when living with synaesthesia. The brain is a sponge sucking in every detail – images, emotions, smells and scents; events become videos in the brain to wind and rewind, each sensory perception stored in a cerebral hard-drive, to be recalled at leisure. To quote other people's categorisations, ranging in intensity and personal interpretations, I'm different, strange, weird, or scary.

The refuge from this hostile world contained books and words from an early age. When I began writing again after a long hiatus, memories returned with a synaesthesia vengeance – vivid in every sense and emotion, including people

I had met or worked with along the way. Whether experiencing first-hand the trauma of refugees fleeing war atrocities, my own difficult and joyous life experiences, or detailed events, I tapped into the hard drive to create stories and novels conveying powerful emotions and environments that gripped readers with their intensity. Sensory writing gave life to the Singapore jungle, the wintery Salisbury Plain of my childhood, and the Caucasus mountains where I once worked. Top agents sent complimentary comments on the quality of my writing but, *"no market for it"*. Despite *"excellent characterisation, gripping plot"*, immersive descriptions of places and *"powerful, evocative and provocative writing"*, I've always chosen unusual locations and themes based on a strong sense of social justice. I followed the advice of 'Write what you want', only to end up as a *"Marmite writer"* with a very distinctive 'voice' but either loved or hated, which made the difference in competitions. Commended, highly commended, never in the top three despite numerous long and shortlists. Always the bridesmaid, never the bride...

Several months before the first Covid lockdown, I'd found money for an ex-commissioning editor of top publishers to mentor my second novel so it could be more commercial. Before accepting he asked to read the totality of my works; first novel, 30k second novel, individual short stories and an historical Anglo-Indian collection previously longlisted for the SI Leeds Prize. He was so impressed that he gave me a discounted price because he couldn't understand why I wasn't already published. I wrote the second novel batch by batch. He'd send his comments and recommendations. I'd then send the edited previous chapters with the new ones. I received continuous glowing compliments, but he said one thing which remains with me: *"As an ex-commissioning editor, I've read hundreds and hundreds of potential books but yours is the first to keep me enthralled and surprised. This is the first novel where I'm excited and curious about how the characters and plot develop in each new batch. Your powerful writing full of unexpected twists keeps me guessing right until the last surprising last few pages."*

The conclusion is – if there's an agent out there who likes Marmite, provocative and atmospheric writing, please get in contact? I'm also working on memoir(s) based on a very interesting and eventful life – another cord to my writing bow.

GAIL BOLLAND

NOTES ON DISCOURAGEMENT
AND COURAGE

I have been invited to contribute to this anthology because I first proposed the idea to Soroptimist International, (SI) Leeds, to fund a literary prize for UK Black and Asian women writers.

I joined the club on retirement. Its members helped me to deliver major arts projects for a new cancer hospital in Leeds. My job had been fundraising for and commissioning multi-arts projects in the acute health sector. I can't take much credit for the concept of a prize. Speaking some French, I became the SI Leeds contact for SI Grenoble, which had already developed a prize for French women writers for whom French was not their first language.

My trade had been developing arts projects, so a literary prize struck me as a good fit for the SI club's aims to support education and career opportunities for women and girls. SI Leeds had the funds to seed such a project and I had contacts with Peepal Tree Press and Ilkley Literature Festival, both of which I thought would find mutual interests in partnering such an initiative.

The prize became one of those blessed projects that lands on its feet: a staunchly committed Chairwoman in Val Saunders, a brilliant coordinator (now Director) in

Fiona Goh who, together with Hannah Bannister at Peepal Tree Press, enrolled a star-studded array of patronnes and, finally, a hugely energetic and creative prize advocate in Irenosen Okojie. But all of this expertise might have gone to waste if it wasn't for those women with knock-out talent, courage and readiness to submit their writing.

I remember a Colombian salsa teacher, Tanya Cusan-Espinosa, urging a hunched class of Leeds 8-year-olds to "Stand as if you are somebody." She embodied what she meant, holding herself tall and proud. Those girls and boys looked uncomfortable, even scared to strike such a pose. Discouragement to *be somebody* comes early in most UK households.

My own discouragements played out in fairly privileged white surroundings. I was the eldest of five daughters born into a farming family that needed a son and heir. My father had been an only boy with three sisters, so inherited the farm along with the misogyny to justify his position, which the culture of the time reflected in every mundane transaction. Dad expounded the superiority of males. As girls, we were not eligible to inherit a farm, nor was any other place in the world indicated for us apart from a marriage that might reflect well on the family.

It turned out that, at 18, I wanted to go to art college. My father, who had shown no interest in my education, didn't even know what A-levels I was doing, took me aside to tell me just how ludicrous was my ambition. "There are no women artists. You can never be an artist," he assured me. I knew this to be untrue, but my own father asserting such a thing dissolved more of my inner self-belief, however rebelliously I acted out.

The farm was a few miles from Wolverhampton and my

youth coincided with Enoch Powell's 'Rivers of Blood' speech with its incitements to attack non-white groups of people as alien, dangerous and unwanted.

Perhaps through my own childhood experience of sexism, I glimpsed the cruelty of racism. My reality was of white, middle-class privilege. It played like a filter over everything but, at times, events and words by writers such as James Baldwin, Angela Davis and other US civil rights activists broke through and enjoined me to their struggle. As I wasn't allowed to go to art college at 18, I initiated a research project to discover what rationale underpinned racist views in Wolverhampton.

With a teenage friend at Wolverhampton Technical College, I devised a questionnaire that could be analysed by the business studies department there, where I had a contact. We took to the streets with clip boards to canvas passers-by, recording their demographic details and answers, all of which could be coded for analysis. I wanted to expose the myths and ignorance that allows one group of people to dehumanise another. I believed then that the published results of our findings would have those who held racist views thinking, "Hey, I got this all wrong. Of course, everyone's equal! We all deserve a fair society." What I actually got was horror from my extended family, a front-page shock exposé in the *Wolverhampton Express & Star* and a bombardment of obscene hate mail, the toxicity of which I could not have imagined, but which was obviously heavily stockpiled and regularly blitzing Black and Asian communities. I felt naïve, isolated and severely discouraged.

I did go to art college but I had to wait until I was twenty-one, then the legal age of independence. I chose to move to

London to do a Fine Art degree and, there, the fog of white male supremacy and empire was thinning in patches. Different realities were being revealed to me, if hazily.

I did well at art college. I was 'promising'. While I lacked self-belief and confidence, I was packed with an energetic passion for the arts. I still do believe the arts are essential for everyone's health, that they put us in touch with the heart of ourselves, that, when they reach us, they give us the truth of experience and the courage to speak and act for justice.

Through the arts, I met women, stronger and more courageous than myself, who helped my glimpse of racial oppression become a little broader. Claudette Johnson (now MBE) was a student at Wolverhampton School of Art, where I did some part-time work. She and I became friends at a time when she and other black artists were beginning to reject the white European aesthetic they were expected to adhere to. Claudette was the main organiser of the first National Black Artists Convention and is now considered one of the finest figurative artists in the UK. Back in the 80s I remember her telling me how exhausting she found it, trying to be a bridge between Black and White communities. I count myself as part of that White community it was so exhausting for Claudette to span and reach any point of real understanding. All privilege is immersed in the experience of its own dominance.

It has taken other encounters, over many years, for me to see how White are our theatres, art galleries, dance and opera companies (just to mention the arts) and what intimidation and exclusion that represents to someone from non-European heritage.

I am quite a shy person, rather an unreliable friend. Early undermining experiences often make socialising daunting and exhausting for me. At the last minute, I may cry off a meeting I was looking forward to because I become filled with the early fear that I am just not good enough. The thing is, I know I am not unique here. My retreat into myself is normal. Anyone who is routinely discouraged as a child, whether by family or the prevailing oppressions of racism, sexism and class will have to expend enormous amounts of energy just to keep their head above water, emotionally and practically. However, solidarity with others facing oppression is the best lifebelt there is.

Background research for the SI Leeds Literary Prize showed that Black and Asian Women writers were woefully under-represented in mainstream publishing, so the format of the prize was created to address that issue. The solidarity of those working to deliver the prize together with the cohort of past shortlisted writers has achieved something remarkable. A peek at the prize website shows how writers who entered for the prize have developed into mature, important literary voices. I go into bookshops now and see their writing displayed within mainstream literature.

I am no longer actively involved in the prize but feel greatly honoured to have been part of its development. I count meeting Margaret Busby and Bonnie Greer, early patronnes of the prize, as one of the highlights of my life.

As a group of elderly white women, SI Leeds took the courage to embark on a project to become effective allies to sisters of different heritage. While the struggle for equality needs to be ongoing on all fronts, the SI Leeds Literary Prize, and all who support it, can say to themselves, "Well done!"

KAVITA A. JINDAL

TO EXPLAIN OR NOT, TO ITALICISE OR NOT

These are the conundrums I frequently get asked about. In addition to writing itself, and writing well, writers whose story-context, setting, culture and climate are different from the country of publication also have to wrestle with decisions about explanations and italicisation. This applies to all writers, and indeed translators, who are straddling two or three cultures but know their readers may not have all the exact same knowledge at their fingertips. The last thing anyone wants to do is alienate readers or patronise them. It's a fine balance, especially these days when there are pushbacks to whatever you choose to do about giving explanations.

For the purposes of this article I'm going to stay within the context of publishing in Britain and focus on the challenges for writers from ethnic-minority backgrounds who are also expressing a non-dominant culture within their work, to a large or small degree, depending on the individual and their narrative. It's a given that the main, or chosen, medium of expression is English and the hoped-for readers and publishers are from the English-centric world – at least at first.

As a first example of a different cultural setting I'll use India, as that's where my novel *Manual For A Decent Life* is set. How far should common perceptions of the country dictate the reader's grasp of your narrative? Do you take into account the reader's likely familiarity or unfamiliarity with cultural conventions *and* how they are broken, as you gallop along with your tale? What if conventions are very different in a metropolitan city and a small village, as is the case with most countries in Asia and Africa.

I confess that many years ago I started out very firmly in the "Do Not explain" camp. Works in English or works translated into English and set, say in South America, did not necessarily need to be "explained" to me; as a faraway reader I absorbed the culture as I read and made what sense of things as I could. So, there wasn't a need for an introduction to Delhi, the city which features in my book. There have been plenty of novels set in Delhi, most of them do manage to bring out the peculiarity of the city: the clashes between it being the axis of political power, the bigwigs and businessmen moving in their rippling circles, the massive population getting by. All the oddities and irregularities of life in the city would come out in the wash, so to speak, as the novel progressed.

Then I came to the stumbling block of interspersing phrases in a local language: Hindi, or even Hindi-English slang, and local syntax, into an otherwise grammatically-correct English text. I am particularly fond of local syntax as I feel it grounds the book in a particular place. Phrases that occur naturally in dialogue logically get included according to me. But trouble brews when local words are used in the main narrative text. There are many tales of mockery about Indian authors who "explained" some "foreign" words, although the actual words were common-place, if the reader ate Indian cuisine for example. In one instance an author was lambasted for clarifying the word 'dal' (cooked lentils) and here I'm doing it too, just in case, you don't know what 'dal' is. Indian-origin authors have been known to take each other to task about such elucidations and then commit a similar "mistake" them-selves. On the food front, I decided mostly not to explain but in two instances added an exposition, as I did for a few other things, sometimes an item of clothing. One of the methods of "explanation" writers use is to carefully tack on a translation soon after, which I did when I wished to translate a Hindi phrase. Other times I slipped in a defini-tion or description of the word used, when there was no way to directly translate. Either way, there is an element of repetition involved for the sake of clarity for those who don't understand the other-language reference. This slows down the text for those readers who grasp everything immediately.

I should declare that in my case there were discussions between Brighthorse Books and myself about what was going to be italicised and what was not. Brighthorse was going to be the first publisher of the book, in a U.S. edition, after my manuscript won their novel prize. Linen Press published the U.K. edition a few months later. I did have some words italicised in my manuscript so it was a continu-ation of a decision I'd already made. It was good to hear that both publishers were happy to leave everything unitalicized if I so wished. In other words, if I wanted to keep everything unexplained for the reader, it was up to me, provided I could explain the text to the publisher whenever they came up against something they weren't sure of. I think this is a fantastic attitude and it's really important that publishers maintain this openness.

When I started out in the "do not explain" camp, this is what I believed: the meaning of the local phrase will eventually be understood by the context of its usage. True, a reader who doesn't know this other language or culture may not get the *literal* meaning but they should be able to get the sense of what was said and why. The reader should be credited with being not only intelligent, but hardworking as a reader!

The person who benefits most from the no italics, no careful add-ons, no glossary approach is the reader who speaks or understands both languages used – English and the local vernacular. That reader, especially if they are absolutely familiar with the context as well, will get a near-indecent thrill from recognising two languages in one sentence and relishing the allusions made. No explanations required, just the joy of seeing the nail being hit on the head. I love that frisson.

And yet. The person who is unacquainted with that particular culture and language cannot enjoy the sentence on the same level. It's not that they are left baffled, but depending on their nature and level of curiosity their reading may stall for a moment and they might resent the intrusion of phrases they don't understand. So should we be spoon-feeding those readers, or to put in corporate-speak: should we be 'creating a smoother reading experience' for them?

As it might be clear I switched camps. This happened because of my experiences as a reader and also as a writer, especially when I was completing final edits on my novel manuscript. I realised that I just wasn't as patient a reader as I'd imagined myself to be. Recently I read a very beautiful poem but felt I'd missed something, possibly I'd missed the main point even, because in the penultimate sentence a Spanish word had been used and I didn't know the meaning of it. It made me cross. Why was I being credited with more knowledge and linguistic skills than I have? Why was I being credited with the dedication to look up this word online, and immediately? Where was the little asterisk at the bottom of the page with the definition of the Spanish word? How could I just skip over this word and yet fully enjoy the poem? It was a striking poem, but surely I'd missed something?

Whenever this happens in poetry, I think that for me knowing the exact meaning of each word matters in a poem. In a longer work it's perhaps less important. It's more about whether enough has been explained. Too many pointers can make the text ungainly.

Many voracious readers will tell you they don't want to be interrupted by a footnote or an indication to flip to the glossary at the back when they are sailing along with their reading. From my recent experience I would say that's half of your readers. And the other half are upset that you didn't think to include a glossary. Time for some more disclosure. I already knew that I would please and displease people in equal measure by "explaining" or "not explaining". So I took the middle route. I slipped in expositions where I saw fit. I did prepare a glossary and mulled over including it. I checked with the publishers who said they didn't think it was necessary. I did get some feedback from readers, after publication, who berated me for not making the text easier for them, although they agreed that not understanding some terminology did not have an impact on them following the narrative.

Which brings me to some interesting developments in

English language poetry, where experimental bilingualism is blossoming. For this article I'll draw my observations from the recent publication *Where Else – An International Hong Kong Poetry Anthology*. The editors say they meant to offer a glimpse into the diverse range of voices that make up the diasporic imagination of the contemporary Hong Kong poetry community. They adopted an approach that encompassed both native Hong Kong writers as well as expatriate and mixed-race voices who were born or have lived in the city, or have strong connections to it. An expansive net resulting in a wide mix of poets, including me. Many of the poems utilise Chinese characters in the text. Some poets have chosen the route of a quick explanation following the Chinese character, others have used footnotes. A couple of poets have dispensed with explanations. They've used local phrases and Chinese characters, and if you know you know, if you don't you don't. Therefore someone like me who may understand the cultural context and the city itself, but who cannot read or speak Chinese has to live with the fact that there is a part of the poem that is not for me. I may still understand the poem with a bit of effort, but I won't get the whole of it on my own; it's not a full round moon for me, as I refer to poems that I won't completely comprehend.

This non-explanation, this leaving of a poem to be elusive to some readers, is a deliberate choice. A statement, in fact, of the poet's place in poetry and their place at these bi-lingual crossing points. It is an example of how experimental forms move literature into new spaces.

Any melding of tongues and civilisations to eventually come across as readable and well written is not easy. Especially in some languages, such as many African languages, rendering a few carefully placed words into English transcription takes a lot of work. In any case, even within related societies there is scope for non-understanding. This holds particularly true of widespread geographical regions and widespread diasporas that we bundle together under an umbrella term for ease of categorisation.

This has always been brought home to me by Indian authors from various states in India who joke (but meaningfully) that they require a glossary for my Delhi idioms (as I would for theirs in their languages), a food dictionary (which I, in turn, might need for their food references) and a note on cultural practices, as they do differ from region to region within the same nation.

To return to the title, "To Explain or Not, To Italicise or Not" instead of an answer I'd like to offer honest advice. The trick may well be asking yourself: How much do I care to explain? Do I want to indicate unfamiliar words with italics? What are my reasons for the decisions I'm making?

Remember, this is your choice as a writer. If you do explain or over-explain, know that there might be someone who will howl about principles or ask for activism against language-colonialism of the past, among other things. There will definitely be a host of others who will appreciate all the indications and information you provide. There also exists the middle route that I took. Which may please no one but you! When preparing the manuscript you should do what feels right and comfortable to you as an author who wants to reach readers. If that is your aim. When it's time for publication, do take into account your publisher's suggestions. They have, after all, closely read the text. The final decisions, dear author, should rest with you.

SUAD KAMARDEEN

UNHEARD STORIES

I have an obsession with documenting stories. When I read, I try to figure out what exactly the author is bearing witness to – a culture or multiplicity of cultures, history, a state of being, a state of living. The more I read, the more I continue to wonder what the book world would look like fifty years from now if the publishing landscape continues the way it's headed. Whose stories will be passed on? Whose books will fill bookshops, libraries and students curricula? What heroes will kids know about and want to embody?

Late last year, I was commissioned to put together a publishing showcase featuring books by Black Muslim authors published in the last two years across genres and age groups. To say I was shocked by how sparse this was, is an understatement. I knew there was no way Black Muslims simply weren't writing, so I dug deeper and stumbled on a world where such writers had resorted to self-publishing or creating their own spaces, after being told far too many times that 'we're not sure how to place or market your story'. What is it about our stories that made them so difficult to place? This is not to say some stories aren't difficult to place but having been on the receiving end of such feedback, I know how subjective, fickle and sometimes 'lazy' the industry can be in its dealing with Black and

Muslim stories. We forget the nuances which exist in the lives of Black Muslims from our upbringing to the richness of our cultures – even within the same country or community, there's diversity and huge range. I think of my immediate circle of Muslim friends with origins from Somalia, Nigeria, Ghana, Egypt, Sudan, Guinea, Yemen, Ethiopia, Comoros Island, Germany, France and much more. Of how distinct their experiences are from mine, and how much I yearn for the stories they have to tell. You could fill volumes and volumes of books with stories centred on these experiences, yet we only get to tell the story publishing wants to see.

Recently, an acquaintance and fellow writer messaged me to ask if there was any point in writing stories centred around Muslim characters who were Black, particularly if they are not focused on 'big' topics like love, race or Islamophobia. She adored authors like Elizabeth Strout, Fredrik Backman, L.M. Montgomery, and wanted to write stories about the everyday mundane life of Black Muslims, but she was also worried about starting the herculean task of writing a novel, only to find that no-one was interested in such stories. I was on the verge of rushing to respond with Toni Morrison's famous quote, 'If there's a book you want to read, but it hasn't been written yet, then you must write it,' but I stopped myself and sat with the question for a while. The publishing world is bleak; it's my current reality, so I understand how difficult it can be to carry that weight. To have all these stories you want to share with the world yet be told that the world isn't interested in your story unless it fits a particular narrative.

When Trump's travel ban was the main conversation in the world, stories by Muslims were in fashion. When

George Floyd was killed and 'Black Lives Matter' was in vogue, publishing wanted Black stories and it didn't matter whether it was trauma-focused, in fact the more trauma the better. But now, the topic in vogue is 'Black joy'. I remember seeing this everywhere and thinking, *Well that's it for you, Suad.* Hear me out: I love Black joy, I live for Black joy, but I can only write what is true to me and this encompasses the heavy subjects too. This is not to say my stories do not include the joy in my characters' lives, but if I had to place them on a scale, the dark slightly outweighs the light. On the basis of this, I've received rejections which made me question whether Black and Muslim writers really have the freedom to tell the stories they want to tell. Sure, the world is bleak enough, but this bleakness remains the lived reality of myself and many others. I understand that my stories may not resonate with everyone, including members of my own community, but I struggle to accept that no-one would want them by virtue of their darkness, when they contain what is universal to the human experience. I'm writing for myself first and foremost, but I also want my stories to reach people. At the same time, I cannot tweak my story to fit a particular mould simply because it's what publishing wants. I don't want my story to only be wanted when it's about the next cool thing.

I've always wanted to be a storyteller and author, but it's taken me some time to work towards bringing this to fruition. I know the stories I want to tell, who my audience are, and I have no intentions of writing for the white gaze. Armed with this knowledge, I realise my publishing journey will be far from smooth sailing. Everyone faces a level of difficulty at different stages of the process, but when you are Black and Muslim, the expectations and limits skyrocket and difficulties abound at every stage. That I'd prepared myself for the difficulty doesn't make it any less frustrating. There always seems to be that 'similar' book or that book which ticks the box, so therefore there can be no other like it in any shape or form. Until said book is published and you realise the only similarity between that book and yours is the race or religion of your protagonists or both.

When I get a version of 'we have that Black story' or 'Muslim story', I have to remind myself of why I started writing in the first place. I also think about how far I've come and all those like me who want to write but may not have the opportunities I've had so far, which allow me to be here. I appreciate and will forever be grateful for the mentorships I've been a part of, but I think of all those who will never make it simply because of the reality of things – these mentorships/opportunities only have a limited capacity (and understandably so).

I've also come to realise that the publishing industry is skilled at tackling symptoms but not root causes. So, between now and whenever we arrive at a place where publishing does right by Black, Muslim and Black Muslim authors, I take it upon myself to remind my fellow brothers and sisters who have been turned down just because, that our stories do matter and Black and Muslim is not a monolith. We have a plethora of valid experiences which we should not tire of writing and shouting about. And if we do get tired, we should just rest and pick up again because our stories do matter, and no-one can ever tell them as we would. There is space in the world for all the versions of our stories that we want to tell, and we deserve to take up space. Our stories will reach those they are meant to reach, and it will resonate beyond our expectations.

My friend, who's also a writer, sends me a voice note at 6:07 in the morning, groggy-voiced because she wanted to apologise for all I'd been going through in trying to be published. She adds a disclaimer that this is not to say she hadn't taken my struggles seriously in the past, but she'd attended an event the night before where a multiple award-winning, best-selling BIPOC author shared similar struggles and was candid about the bleakness in the publishing industry for BIPOC authors, and it really put things into perspective for her. It felt good to be seen and heard and understood and validated. Her message was just what I needed in that moment, just the push to surge forward. And it made me further appreciate how pivotal community has been to my experience in the writerly world. I can carry on because I am continuously affirmed by a community of people – living and dead – who remind me that they see me.

I think now of my experience doing a reading of my YA novel (which won the 2022 SI Leeds Literary Prize) at an event filled by Black and Asian people and being told by people in the audience how much the story resonated with them, and how they couldn't wait to see it out in the world. Months later, people reach out to me to find out when the book will be ready to purchase because they have cousins, daughters, nieces and friends whom they would like to share it with. These moments are some of the moments I hold most dear because they remind me of some of the reasons why I do what I do. Even though publishing says, 'I'm not sure where to place your book' or 'we couldn't emotionally connect with your characters', I know that there are people who will connect and love it enough to want to pass on.

SUMANA KHAN

THE ACT OF READING

When the email from SI Leeds dropped in my inbox asking if I'd be interested in contributing an essay for this anthology, I agreed without batting an eyelid. And then the air traffic mayhem unfolded. I panicked mildly as I waited in a crowded airport for my delayed return flight – an essay was due… It was déjà vu from my student days. I almost heard my class teacher's voice in my head – as a punishment Sister J would have asked me to submit a 500-word critique of the novel I was currently reading. I won't… don't critique Jack Reacher. But I guess I will dedicate this essay to the one lifelong habit I have – reading.

I grew up in Bengaluru, India. Back in the 1980s the city was leafy, not a single apartment high-rise blighted the skyline, and a majority of us were from "lower middle-class" i.e. working class families. This meant that most of us did not own a car; none of us had telephone connections (it was rotary) except for the rich who resided in properties they owned; and most of us did not own television sets – television manufacturing hadn't started in full steam in India. Only "upper middle-class" folks owned black and white TV sets in the early 1980s.

The most accessible form of entertainment for us was reading books. There was this weird library near my home…

my own Narnia. The place was a windowless shop, probably 10 x 10 feet. Books were simply piled up against the walls and heaped all over the floor. There was not a single piece of furniture, except for a foldable aluminium chair on which the owner sat, a man with droopy eyes and longish hair. There was no evidence of any library system – no library membership cards, not even a ledger in sight where the man kept track of the books. But it soon became clear to us patrons that the library system was recorded and mapped in the man's brain. Tell him a title and he would extract it from the pile of hundreds of books within a second. He knew exactly which books you took and which ones you returned. And all the time he would be perched on his chair, legs crossed, reading a daily.

So as a pre-teen, my holidays and weekends were well-stocked with comics. I was crazy about Indrajal comics who published Phantom, Mandrake, and Flash Gordon strips, and with Enid Blyton books because that's what my friends at my all-girls Catholic school were reading. We were forming our own versions of Famous Five and Secret Seven clubs, acting all mysterious, and after a big phase of St Clare's, we wondered if our parents would allow us to go to a boarding school.

And then someone discovered Nancy Drew. I rushed to my library. 'Growing up fast, eh?' Library Uncle said and handed over a bunch of Nancy Drew and Hardy Boys mysteries. Yes, we all felt pretty grown up – we now knew that a "date" did not necessarily mean a calendar number or a dry fruit. But our sense of superiority did not last long because we were outdone by a classmate. We had a free period and our class teacher asked if anyone wanted to tell a story. This classmate, I'll refer to her as P, volunteered.

We all perked up. P was *the* best story narrator in the batch, and she was probably going to narrate Nancy Drew's *The Kachina Doll Mystery*... Not many of us had access to a copy yet.

But P began, "This is about a man who was hired to assassinate the French President Charles De Gaulle." The next period was cancelled – we all wanted to know, including our class teacher, who won this cat and mouse chase – the Jackal or Lebel?

That evening I opened the atlas and sat studying Europe (Amma thought I had a geography test that I'd neglected till the last minute). I was trying to trace the countries through which the Jackal had traversed, I found it incredible that you could just drive from one country to another in Europe; I couldn't even imagine travelling from Bengaluru to Delhi.

Library Uncle shook his head vehemently when I asked for the book. It had adult content. 'At your age you must laugh,' he said and handed over a P.G.Wodehouse – *Piccadilly Jim* if I remember correctly. Then he muttered under his breath, 'What to do... It is the 80s and you children are too fast these days.' I did manage to lay my hands on the book months later; I think the first French words I learned were not 'Salut, ça va' but 'Ici chacal'.

I think what you read in those formative years becomes your lifelong preference. Given a choice I will always pick up genre fiction first... especially crime, thriller, horror. Over the course of years I've had reading phases: for example there were cycles where I read nothing but classics or nothing but non-fiction. But genre fiction is my comfort food... my aloo subzi for the soul.

There is no doubt that I (and my classmates) grew up in

considerable privilege (intellectual, if not material). Having access to books, having an ecosystem of adults who encourage you to read – this should ideally be a norm and not a privilege. But access to books remains a matter of privilege or its absence because it is monitored, curtailed, censored. I have friends whose conservative parents never allowed them to read fiction unless it was a prescribed textbook. Parents feared that reading novels, especially English ones, led to moral corruption (yeah… eye-roll), resulting in poor academic performance, ruining the kid's future, which essentially meant the child would not become an engineer or a doctor – and forget about an officer in the prestigious Indian Administrative Service.

You'd be surprised to know that even this simple act of reading – one of the most non-obtrusive, meditative, and solitary activities – can provoke a range of reactions in an onlooker – from curiosity to aggression. As an Indian woman I've received a variety of unsolicited comments, suggesting that I am probably poor at my job because I'm always "in la-la land" and that I'll turn out to be a hopeless wife… because I'll apparently neglect everyone with my reading. Some of my friends were advised not to reveal their reading hobbies during potential arranged marriage discussions. No one wanted a smartass of a daughter-in-law – especially one who read English books.

One of my most unforgettable conversations was during a work commute. Our office bus was stuck in a traffic jam as usual. A senior colleague sitting across the aisle interrupted my reading and waved his copy of Stephen Covey's *The 7 Habits of Highly Effective People* – a book that I wouldn't touch with a bargepole. Nothing against the book at all, it's just not my cup of tea. 'You should be reading this if you are serious about your career,' the colleague said. And then he added that he was 'telling for my own good.'

I smiled and nodded, hoping that would be the end of it.

He wouldn't let it rest though. Tell me *one* useful thing you learned from that fiction you are reading, he demanded.

'Just from this page I'm on... I've learned that anyone who annoys me, I can saw open their cranium and yet keep them alive, then I can sit that person down at the dining table, remove an edible piece of the brain, cook it fresh and feed it to guests, while Bach plays in the background. How's that for being a highly effective person?'

I narrated this to Amma later that evening. Why does it bother people so much to see a girl reading, I complained. This colleague had nothing to say to another male colleague who was reading an Irving Wallace.

Because, reading makes you think, Amma said. Thinking makes you question. Questioning makes you break the status quo. And nothing is as intimidating as a woman who breaks the status quo... even if it is a small act of stopping someone's intrusion into your mental space.

The process of reading is a very self-centred activity. This is something you do for your own pleasure, out of your own volition. You pick the book, you read at your pace, you *choose not to interact with people and withdraw emotional services*. Whatever the book offers – the entertainment, the mental satisfaction, the soul-nourishment, maybe even boredom – it's all yours, and yours alone. And when you come from a culture where such self-love is discouraged, where femininity is defined by selfless service, every time you pick up a book – it doesn't matter if the book is about an evil killer clown who gobbles up children, or an ex-army guy who travels by bus with just his toothbrush... or hell, even programming in Python – know that you are breaking the status quo.

Go on. Pick up a book.

WINNIE M. LI

THE OPTICS AND THE STORY: ON BEING PUBLISHED AND MARKETED AS AN ASIAN WRITER

In Spring 2018, I was flown to Seoul to launch the Korean edition of my debut novel, *Dark Chapter*. My publisher, Hangilsa Press, had astutely monitored the growing public response to #MeToo in Korea and had decided to not only bring forward my novel's publication date, but also set up a full promotional 'tour' for me with multiple TV interviews, public talks, and a press conference. In some ways, it was every debut author's dream: a round-trip flight halfway across the world, 5 nights in a luxury hotel, guest of honor treatment throughout. It was also completely exhausting, requiring nonstop eloquence and enthusiasm about a difficult topic (my own rape) – and all this while jet-lagged, surrounded by translators.

It was simultaneously exhilarating and lonely, yet also the kind of publicity platform any ambitious novelist would love to have. But throughout most of this, a question popped up – the inverse of a more familiar one: would my Korean publishers have done this if I were white?

I imagine most people of colour living in the West have internally teased a question like that at various points in their lives: would I have been treated like that if I weren't Black? Would those strangers have said that to me if I weren't Asian? Would I have gotten the job if I fitted more easily into the mainstream culture – i.e., if I were white? Most times, the question is posed in reaction to a sense of loss or discrimination. But this time, there was a very unfamiliar notion of privilege: that my publisher was generating this much publicity for my book, precisely because I was a diasporic Asian.

I am not Korean-American. My parents emigrated to the United States from Taiwan. Growing up in New Jersey in the 1980s and 1990s, I never learned to speak Taiwanese or Mandarin. Most of my friends were white, so I was more interested in assimilating into Western white culture than in learning a language that would further set me apart. I learned Spanish and Latin in high school, German in college, French as an adult. I've since lived and worked in Europe, the Middle East, and even Singapore for a 6-month stint – but Asian languages are not something I've successfully managed to grasp.

And yet, this language gap seemed not to be a problem for my Korean publisher. Perhaps for diaspora writers in the West, countries close to their ethnic origins can be a big, sometimes even bigger, market than the original language market. *Dark Chapter* struggled to find a U.S. publisher. In 2015, when it was on submission, many publishers were disturbed by its portrayal of sexual violence, which some editors considered 'too real' or 'too unflinching.' (An ironic comment, given how much some genres rely on sexual violence as a trope.) But the exact opposite happened in Taiwan in Autumn 2017, after my novel won *The Guardian's* Not The Booker Prize. There, a five-way auction for

Complex Chinese rights led to my biggest advance thus far. Of course, my sub-agent made sure to highlight the fact that my parents were Taiwanese immigrants to America, as well as the book's relevance to the #MeToo movement – and where before had we read a #MeToo story where the heroine was Asian?

For writers of colour, the very thing (our ethnicity) which may be a disadvantage to getting published in the West can be a benefit in other parts of the world. I sometimes reshape that familiar question to ask: Would *Dark Chapter* have struggled to find a publisher in the U.S. if I were white? And I honestly do not know the answer. But I look at other writers of colour who are published in the West and how so much of their work deals directly with questions of racial identity, ethnicity, and the immigrant experience – as if that is the only turf allowed to us. Perhaps writers of colour in the West aren't granted the same freedom that white writers have. And Western publishers are only now starting to allow us the same breadth of exploration in subject matter that Barbara Kingsolver or Jodi Picoult or Stephen King take for granted.

You could argue *Dark Chapter* still falls within a tradition of 'pain narratives' expected of writers of colour by Western readers. However, my book doesn't directly address issues of race, even though the heroine's identity as Asian-American informs her experience of the world. It is more a story of gender and class. Interestingly enough, it is only in the U.S., the UK, and Italy where the book is being marketed primarily as a crime novel, using the commercial safety-net of a popular genre. In nearly all the other twelve territories sold, my novel is being positioned as either literary or women's upmarket fiction, with the emphasis on me as a

Taiwanese-American author. If my book were more overtly Asian (instead of inhabiting the amalgamated, international background that I come from), would American and British publishers have known how to market it more easily as literary fiction? If writers like Lisa Ko, Chang-Rae Lee, and Amy Tan address the immigrant experience, are all writers with Asian last names expected to as well?

The Taiwanese edition of my *Dark Chapter* came out in April 2019. Rights for a Mainland Chinese edition sold for more than twice the Taiwanese advance. Indeed, the total advances from my three Asian publishers exceed the total advances from my nine Western publishers. I can't help but notice that the only publishers to have invested in a promotional tour thus far are Asian. I believe it meant something to potential readers in Korea – specifically female readers – to see an author who looked like them. As if our shared experience of womanhood, gender inequality, and (for some) sexual assault, somehow felt closer to theirs because we were the same race.

Nominated for an Edgar Award in 2018, *Dark Chapter* is a fictionalized retelling of my own real-life stranger rape, but imagined equally from the perspectives of both the victim (a character with strong parallels to myself) and the perpetrator (in real life, an Irish teenager who stalked me in a park). It is set largely in Northern Ireland (where my rape took place) and London (where I lived at the time, and primarily still do), so there is no direct connection with contemporary Korean or Asian culture, save for the fact that the victim, Vivian, is Taiwanese-American.

But even this representation of Asian womanhood seemed to be something Korean women readers identified with, particularly around a subject that carries such a cultural taboo. During my promotional tour, Korean women lined up at the signing table, some of them sharing their own stories of sexual trauma with me. Some would cry, telling me how grateful they were I had written this book. My literary translator, Byeol Song, is herself a rape survivor and public about this – and I, in turn, was grateful for the emotional authenticity she gave to the Korean edition. Elsewhere on my tour, I conversed with leading feminist scholar Dr. HyunYoung Kwon-Kim, participated in a special discussion with women journalists, gave a lecture for Women's Studies Masters programme, delivered a TED-style televised talk. At night in my hotel room, I cried on my own – partly out of sheer exhaustion, partly out of the chance to connect with these women living on the other side of the world, Korean readers I wouldn't have otherwise met.

In some ways, I am accustomed to this kind of emotional labour. In my professional life in the UK, enabling conversations with other rape survivors is part of my day-to-day work. I founded a festival that addresses sexual assault through the arts and discussion, and I work with a charity on improving media coverage of these experiences. I often don't earn much money for these efforts, but I approach them on a professional level, as I consider the work to be so necessary. In the UK, I am often one of few ethnic minorities in a predominantly white, middle-class world of activists and public rape survivors. In these situations, it is often my American-ness which comes to the fore: my willingness to talk openly about a very private experience, my ease at public speaking honed by a childhood of 'Show and Tell' and after-school debate clubs).

Because sexual assault is so deeply personal, do people naturally feel drawn to someone whose experience *seems* closer to theirs – because of how they look? If I were white and talking about my rape, would Korean readers have thought my life experience was too different from theirs to relate to, despite also being a rape survivor? I never felt comfortable asking this question aloud, but I often wondered if a racial difference between reader and author creates a perceived gap for publishers, even though literature is meant to transcend these human particularities. As a Taiwanese-American girl growing up in the US, I certainly identified with characters who didn't come from a world anything like mine: Huckleberry Finn, Holden Caulfield, Bigger Thomas. And indeed, it works the other way around. I've had white male readers say that reading *Dark Chapter* made them understand a bit better what it's like to be a woman, who cried reading the scenes of the heroine's experience of the criminal justice system. So if they can identify with a Taiwanese-American heroine, then that's already one step towards progress.

But nevertheless, barriers persist, even if erected by publishers trying to market an author for the public. It was strange – and a bit sad – trying to explain this predicament to Korean audiences. Trying to explain to a near-homogenous society (where race is taken for granted) that in the West, your race as an Asian could set you apart in a negative way. I said that there were few Asian women with a public profile in the West. And Asian writers were often expected to write about 'being Asian', rather than a more 'universal' experience like gender or sexual assault.

It was the first time I felt I could even mention that publicly when discussing the book. As if voicing those thoughts to a more general, Western audience might label me a whiney or ungracious minority writer. In Korea, I sensed a duty to be honest about it. About the kinds of unspoken discriminations that still happen to women of colour in the West, in 2018. If Asians have an image of America or the UK as being places of opportunity, I felt compelled to specify that those opportunities are still limited, depending on your ethnicity.

I wonder why I told them that. Perhaps I myself perceived a sense of kinship with these Asian women. Perhaps we are all susceptible to this desire to bond with people who look like us. The optics affect all of us – even the most cynical – into an imagined sympathy. And yes, visibility matters. Even a symbolic visibility enables an author to connect with an audience.

It's been fascinating to see how my Taiwanese and Chinese publishers handled *Dark Chapter*. (Of the eleven book covers by international publishers, only the Dutch one explicitly shows an Asian face in the cover design). My Mainland Chinese publisher has invited me to Beijing to promote the forthcoming Complex Chinese edition. A British-Vietnamese producer is optioning the film rights. And, as I write my second novel, I also wonder if it's a disadvantage with Western publishers that my work doesn't address ethnic identity more explicitly. Should I write what's easier to market by an Asian diaspora author, or what truly interests me? Of course, it's the latter. As I've been told time and time again by other writers, you just have to hope your work will find its readers. Regardless of your race and theirs.

This essay was originally published on the Electric Literature website in Spring 2019, after the international publication of Winnie's debut novel *Dark Chapter* (2nd place, SI Leeds Literary Prize 2016).

WENYAN LU

MY WRITING 'ROOM'

I always wanted to be a writer, as early as when I was a child. Yes, it does sound like a cliché. But I never told anyone. It almost sounds wrong if you say you want to be a writer. *'Why can't you get a proper job?'* people would say to you.

I didn't become a writer when I was old enough to get a 'proper job'. I became a teacher, and for a once-ambitious person, it was a bit too ordinary a job. I was then offered a job at a radio station, so I actually started writing a lot. I was happy enough, but I sometimes asked myself whether I wanted to be a 'proper' writer, writing stories for myself, not for work.

Then one day, before I knew it, I had moved to the UK.

I became a full-time housewife, with two young children. Suddenly, there were no ambitions left for me to fulfil. Well, there was one, or even two ambitions perhaps – to be a good mother and wife. I never undermine housewives, and I might have done a wonderful job of being one of them. Since the daytime was tiring and hectic, I only had some time to myself after the children went to bed when I could sit in bed for a while before I went to sleep. It was a precious two-hours-ish of time. My husband was studying for a master's, so he was usually reading papers or writing his essays. I had a pile of books too, mostly novels, on the bedside table. I would read until I felt sleepy. I fell asleep and entered my dreams with some of the words of those novels ingrained in my head.

When I look back, I feel grateful to my husband for encouraging me to do what I liked and wanted to do. I was also lucky I didn't need to take English courses like a lot of new immigrants since I was an experienced English teacher and established translator in Shanghai before I met my husband. While I was doing a lot of reading, the urge to write returned. I wanted to communicate with the world – I wanted to tell my stories.

I didn't have *a room of my own* for writing like Virginia Woolf's idea in the 1920s for female writers. What I gathered was that the room was more about a woman's independence and space. What she referred to didn't have to be a physical room; it was somewhere you felt free and secure and it didn't require approval from men, or anyone else. Equipped with a free spirit, a woman, or anyone, would be able to express themselves. But I did have that *room of my own*, which was my family, where I could talk with the power of my pen.

I could write, but I wanted to write better, so I wanted to learn how to write better. Soon I discovered that the UK was a land of learning, life-long learning. Perhaps it wasn't too late to start something new?

My husband encouraged me to sign up for writing courses. He looked after our two little children when I went to my class in the evening. My confidence gradually built up and I went on to study for a Master of Studies in Creative Writing at the University of Cambridge.

I was the only student on the Master's course who had an Asian heritage, but I didn't feel left out. There was a respectful and sincere atmosphere. What I learnt from the course was not only the craft of writing, but also what to write and how to express emotions freely with your own style and point of view. That was where I found another writing 'room' for myself, where my voice could be heard. The most important thing I learned was being truthful and genuine when you write – you only write what you really think.

Writing is creating. It's never easy. Sometimes it seems impossible for someone like me, who writes in English as a second language and who is relatively new in the UK, to be published. There is a long distance between 'impossible' and 'possible'. You do your work and try your best, then the distance will shrink over time until the 'impossible' and 'possible' meet.

There are a lot of writing competitions out there, so I started entering competitions. Nobody knew who I was, which made me feel relaxed, since entries were blind-read. Competitions helped me improve my editing skills, and most importantly, to be disciplined in order to meet deadlines; after a couple of attempts, I found myself being longlisted by competitions, then eventually won. But there was still a long way to go to get published.

I didn't give up. I didn't know where my dedication would take me, and I didn't mind. All I did was write, and keep writing. In the end, my 'impossible' and 'possible' met after nearly ten years' resilience, in the 'room' where my creativity took flight.

Today, I still don't have a writing room of my own. I don't plan to have one. I don't need one, either. I can write anywhere. I don't need to be provided with any external space. My strength comes from within.

All you need for writing is a 'room', and it is free.

AMITA MURRAY

UNLADYLIKE MUSINGS ON WRITING, RACE AND SEX

Promoting my first Regency novel, *Unladylike Lessons in Love* (HarperCollins), is a surreal experience. The more I want to plug it as one of the few (if not, in fact, *the* only) Regency novels that explores colonial history and slavery, the more I seem to be trending in historical erotic fiction, and a category I'd never heard of before but that opens up mind-boggling vistas: humorous erotica.

This series of novels is about the Marleigh sisters, daughters of an English earl and his Indian mistress. In the 1700s, men of the East India Company spread their wings (and not just their wings) far and wide in India. As Empire spread, this trading company fast annexed large parts of India, dominated its trade and plundered Indian wealth. In the 1700s and early 1800s, men of the East India Company were more likely to assimilate, more likely to take on 'native' wives and mistresses. Some of the children of these unions were sent to England to get an education and make a life. This history forms the basis of the Marleigh Sisters series.

Romance fiction is supposed to be frothy and fun. It's supposed to be a pleasant and sweet escape. Yet, how can I, a writer-of-colour, write Regency fiction about mixed-race protagonists and yet make them the same benign works of fiction about marriage mart virgins as everyone else? The answer is I can't. If I write historical fiction, then I *have to* write about colonial history, slavery, the abolitionists and, yes, racism. I can't escape those themes.

In this Regency series, not only do we have the backstory of Lila and her sisters – how did they end up in England? What happened to their parents out in India? – but each book dwells on a mystery, often with a backdrop in the 'colonies'. If we want to make space for writers-of-colour to enter the field of commercial and commercially-viable fiction, we have to not just open the door to them, but allow them to *change and evolve the stories we think we know*.

That said, there are two things important to me when I am writing this series. The question of colonial history and its impact on the changing population of the UK. The second is the question of South Asian women and sexuality. Sexless stereotypes of South Asian women abound in the media and in novels. In the United States, there are women like Priyanka Chopra and Mindy Kaling who portray women with sexual desires and sexual agency. *Bridgerton*, too, has done what it can to bring us South Asian love interests. But in UK media, stereotypes of arranged marriage, traditional family structures, and South Asian women as sexless doctors and lawyers aren't easy to shake.

In *Unladylike Lessons*, the protagonist, Lila Marleigh, embraces the two sides of her identity, Indian and English. But more importantly, in portraying her, I consciously steered clear of Regency tropes of virginity *and* stereotypes of South Asian women as sexual victims. Stories of oppression are vital to tell and we must make space for them. But where are the women who experience passion and desire, who have sexual agency, who take their lives and passions into their own hands? Why can't I find these women if I look in the media and in books? Why, when I read novels, can I find white and black women, and increasingly women from East Asia, who are healthy, sexual beings, but I can't find these stories for South Asian women? Why can't we tell a whole array of diverse stories and not confine ourselves only to recognisable and palatable Orientalist stereotypes?

The Marleigh Sisters series tries to change these harmful stereotypes, expanding the repertoire of stories available to South Asian women. Of course, in the meantime, I'm laughing out loud at my current Number One slot in the Kindle bestseller lists in historical erotic fiction, Victorian erotica and humorous erotica. Because you know what? It's about time women of colour get to define their sexuality and take it into their own hands. My books will keep on trying to do just that.

IRENOSEN OKOJIE

THREE WISE WOMEN

That period I call winter, when life seemed unbearable and I found myself crying silently on peripheries slightly beyond the city, I thought about being unwittingly complicit in the disappearance of a woman I used to know. Who looked just like me. What I had left were her excavated bones, which I was forcing myself to survey in order to kick start my own resurrection.

My mother used to tell me the story of how I'd nearly died as a baby. She would always mention this anecdote randomly, uncannily, whenever I was in good spirits as if to remind me to appreciate the chance I'd been given and to warn me of dangers lurking round corners. I'd suffered from convulsions frequently as a baby. Nobody knew what caused them but they were very concerning to my mother and occasionally terrifying for her. In one instance, I convulsed so badly I became unusually still, dead-eyed, quiet. My mother tried everything to revive me but nothing seemed to work. It had been an unbearably hot afternoon, she said, and in the evening, the moon, ironically, appeared even more beautiful.

This was in Benin, Nigeria. We were staying in the rural parts and the nearest hospital was at least a two-hour drive away. My father was out of the country on a business trip. There was no time. Panicked, a little out of her mind, my mother took me to her mother, who tied me on her back. Together, the two carried me to the local river, rushing down the long road in a temperamental white Volkswagen Beetle until they got to the banks, where they waded into the water with me, and my grandmother reached under the surface and fed me something, some weed or part of a plant, which saved me. Many years later, when winter arrived and sucked me into its bleak depths, I thought about that image a lot: three generations of women in the water at night; an intervention, the moon as a witness.

Now grandmother was gone, my mother had her own worries. The first few days of my winter, the start of a long period with no change, I became obsessed with finding out what my grandmother had fed me to revive me. I was fixated on that small detail. I sat in train carriages watching for a far-flung white Calla lily to manifest from a rip in a seat; I wandered through museums hoping for African seaweed to spill through my pockets; I loitered in the waiting room of my local GP longing to catch some wayward water creature through the rhythm in my chest, a creature my grandmother had sent to me from beyond the grave that had only moments left to breathe in the cloistered air of the surgery. But my grandmother had taken her secret with her, and having lived away in England since I was eight, I never thought to ask: the folly of youth. Not even my mother knew. This devastated me as a succession of traumas over the previous years had cast me into a broken place, a seemingly immovable purgatory.

Despite all my efforts to remain optimistic, I was sick. I felt hollowed out, as if my entrails were floating around the city waiting for someone to hold them. I battled a terrible lethargy, couldn't sleep, my back hurt from stress and pres-sure. A searing pain shot through my chest whenever I stepped outside. A cycle of negative thoughts spun on a loop in my head and I couldn't take in the beauty of anything. The frenetic pace of living in London made it hard to pause, to appreciate the glorious light between women passing in animated conversations, the knowing gaze of a fox tailing me at night when I circled our area for a rush of cold air, the poetry of untied shoes in park trees.

I ran. I walked the dog every day. I attended a Buddhist meeting with a friend – an illuminating experience filled with angry, anarchic Buddhists arguing and interrogating what they deemed the failing of their religion to support the disenfranchised. It was wonderful to see, although I felt removed from it because I felt removed from everything during that time. At the height of my anxiety, when it really took hold of my body, I had to cancel the first speaking events for the publication of my debut short story collection – doubly traumatic as I'd worked hard for many years to reach that point.

Jungian psychoanalyst, poet and cantadora Clarissa Pinkola Estes argues that when a woman experiences a gutting we must tap into our wildish nature. That we must leap into that desert or into the snow, and run hard, searching under, searching over, for a sign that she still lives. And that when women reclaim their relationship with the wildish nature, 'they are gifted with a permanent and internal watcher, a knower, a visionary, an oracle, an inspiratrice, an intuitive, a maker, a creator, an inventor, and a listener who guide, suggest, and urge vibrant life in the inner and outer worlds'. I returned to this quote many times during those difficult days. It was to me a rallying cry urging a woman to reach for her true self underneath all the pain of brokenness, to try not to escape that pain but to know it, sit with it, understand it, use it as fuel, then pass through it. I had to seek that internal watcher who would guide me. I had to call to her with a wild cry of my own, feel my warrior heart beating again, let the footprints of

ancestors disintegrate in my blood. I just had to move.
                                    ★
Later that year, I travelled to Berlin for a week to run a
workshop and speak at a salon event. I was struggling with
imposter syndrome exacerbated by my high levels of anxiety.
The room I rented was an efficient, kooky space overlooking
the courtyard of an art gallery compound in Kreuzberg. The
front door to that side of the building was stiff and never
opened properly at first so you had to really lean into it. It was
the same with my room door. This seemed metaphorical to
me, reflective of how, as a black woman in the UK, I had to lean
into spaces and put my full body weight into opportunities in
order to break them open for myself. All the doors on each
floor looked exactly the same. I kept going up to the wrong
floor and leaning in to the wrong door to the bewilderment of
some patient tenant who'd open her door to find me fumbling
with the knob on the other side.

My room was cold. The radiator didn't work properly. At
intervals, it made a thumping noise as if a stone was trapped
inside it. The internet was dodgy. I outdid a contortionist to
get moments of access to awkward corners. Anxiety crept in
incrementally prior to taking hold. A day before my workshop, I was in full panic mode. By then my room was freezing
and I paced back and forth trying not to crawl up the walls.
What could I offer a group of emerging writers when I was
myself falling apart? I decided to roam around the neighbourhood and let it soak up my anxious energy. I took a small
notebook to jot down observations and distract myself as I
walked up to the canal and then widened my exploration. I
loved Berlin. I felt stubborn, determined for things to go well.
And luckily, on that occasion they did.
                                    ★
The complex intermingling of pain and relief in art was

something I constantly grappled with. It was unending, impossible to measure, a bit like time and space in continuum. I only knew that for as long as I could remember, I had always seen art as a transformative space, but true transformation comes with pain, with sacrifice, with the commitment to take a leap of faith when you do not know how you will land, with the kind of loneliness that over time becomes embedded into your DNA. For me, making art, writing in particular, was a long period of incubation and my books were languages waiting to be released, slowly forming and shaping as I felt my way through the dark, catching bits of splintered light I then bent into handwriting on the page, giving communion to characters I could not shake off, carrying their dialogue in my brain like alien infiltrations, promising to know them, to leave markings over their web-like tapestries with curled fingers.

The writing life was harder than anyone had ever told me it would be. It was getting up at dawn to face a blank page when you were unsure of what you'd written two pages before; it was having nobody to guide you because in those early years much of it was hidden, secretive. I could not say I was an author because there was no finished product to show people, no book to proudly place in the hands of others, who eyed me with amusement. Writing meant awkward pauses in conversations with people who did not care for it or understood the tumultuous nature of craft. It meant excruciating periods of waiting for what I deemed my inadequacies to improve. It meant retreating from friends to develop my writing, to live it, breathe it, envision it and make it indelible. It was, and is, a selfish endeavour, yet wholly necessary for me to function, a shared rhythm between brain and hand.

During those lonely days, the writing was a thing of wonder when it began to fall into place, when ideas came effortlessly, when a scene felt right or a character became so fully dimensional that it seemed like I was keeping her company. The joy of creating and moving through worlds was unlike any other pleasure I had ever known. It was addictive. It showed me the possibilities of language, of reaching beyond perceived limitations and into myself. Writing was something I grasped for when the world was spinning around me and nothing made sense. All I ever hoped to do was touch people, move them, make them re-examine trauma, empathy and pain by holding a lens to characters on the fringes. When I struggled, I wrote, so I could try to access the sea under the sea, the clear waters my grandmother had used to give me life again all those years before.

In her book *Bluets*, author Maggie Nelson explores her fascination with the colour blue, how it winds its way through depression, divinity, desire. And how 'each blue object could be a kind of burning bush, a secret code meant for a single agent, an X on a map… that contains the knowable universe'. My winter had been a kind of muted silvery hue, mutating objects to a dull grey around me. From Nelson's quote, I interpreted that 'each blue object'– or grey object, in my case – could be a small revelation, a way of seeing through the fog. And so, a grey day was an indication to take time out for myself, maybe sit in a botanical garden somewhere and try to identify the flowers. A grey reflection in my mirror meant shifting the focus away from myself and treating a loved one to a gift. When apples became grey, it was time to eat rambutan. I took Nelson's lines to mean watching for the signs around me, paying attention and responding in kind so I felt I had some agency and was not completely consumed by the darkness swirling around me.

The crazy thing about all this is that I somehow managed to write two books through this period of silver and grey. For years, writing was a ritual for me, a survival mechanism that had become ingrained into my very core. I had a complicated relationship with it. It was a space I protected fiercely through different career paths, tenuous relationships, family commitments. I needed to make things, to create worlds. I knew how to do that. I don't know if the writing saved me, but it kept me focused. I was driven. I needed something to show for this time of wreckage, something I could weigh, measure, and hold up to the splinters of light occasionally seeping through to say *look at the silver I produced through the fog*. I needed concrete achievements beyond the nebulous black smoke that had first dogged my heels before spiralling through my body.

The final time I saw my grandmother was several months before she died. I was the last grandchild to see her alive. She was moving about with a walking stick, having suffered two strokes and changed drastically with age, but she still had that old magic about her, that free spirit and wilful glint in her eyes. Even then, I forgot to ask what she'd given me from the river. I forgot to say thank you for saving my life. We broke bread, looked at old photographs, danced and drank palm wine together. We had the same arms, the same hands, the same buoyant disposition at our best. I cried on the plane back to London thinking about it.

*

Maybe you wonder what wise women the title of this essay alludes to. Perhaps it's my grandmother, my mother and me. Or maybe it's my grandmother, Clarissa Pinkola Estes and Maggie Nelson, women from different cultures who've mined their experiences to show us the shape of light lurking beneath. Perhaps it's me as a baby, me as a young girl and me now, still finding my way. Or maybe it's three wise women inside all women, speaking to us from the bottom of a river, waiting for us with silvery gifts so we can revive ourselves when winter arrives again.

YOANNA PAK

AND THEN THE ZOMBIES CAME

They pulled him out black and blue. He was covered in blood and his head was so swollen it was misshapen. They feigned joy: "Ooh! Look! He's finally decided to come out! Take a photo!" But they didn't give him to me to hold. They didn't let me feel my baby on my skin, let him match his breathing to mine. They gave him to my husband. To the sounds of newborn screams and desperate attempts of "shush" from my husband, I fell asleep.

The third pull. He finally came out on the third pull. If he hadn't, they would've shoved him back up to do an emergency c-section. Those stories came out after the birth. "I knew of someone whose baby was decapitated with forceps…"; "I know someone who was brain-damaged by forceps and needs constant care…"; "Thank God I didn't let anyone touch my baby with forceps!"

Those stories stay hidden in prenatal classes. They tell you how to avoid using an epidural, how to breathe your child into the world, how to ask for a birthing pool and how important it is to have skin to skin with your baby as soon as they are born.

They were stitching me up for over two hours. I was in and out. There was no skin to skin.

"Oh, yeah, sure, I ripped front to back." Another story that came out later on. Would I have done more Kegels? Probably not. But more olive oil massages? Most definitely yes. Ripped front to back. Sounds horrible, something that should not be mentioned along with the miracle of childbirth, but yes, front to back would be the most accurate description.

My mother had three children vaginally. My sister had hers with no medication and even had a planned home birth. Me? I was filled with pregnancy hubris. I would be just like them. Why not? My mother would tell me that we were meant to have babies. That was my role in life. Marry a Korean-Christian man and have Korean-Christian babies. That was in my twenties, then in my thirties I decided I did not need to get married or have children. The horror! The relief that followed when I finally married a man – even though he was neither Korean nor Christian and didn't even live in Toronto! Worse, he wasn't even Canadian. He lived in London, in the United Kingdom, an entire ocean away. Still, better to be married than alone. There was celebration. The pregnancy came quickly. The marriage was God-ordained! The greatest blessing of all, a child was on its way.

But the birth, oh the birth. All the 'good' advice said to give birth naturally. There are bacteria in the vaginal canal that are essential for the good health of the baby. They cannot reap all these benefits if they bypass the vaginal canal. My baby came out vaginally, but I would never call it a natural birth. From the moment he was induced at 42 weeks to the 72 hours of labour, it stopped being natural. If natural selection had not been usurped by science, it would have bypassed me. I would not have been selected. I should not have followed in the footsteps of my mother and my sister. I was not a natural mother.

As my body healed, I did not.

They do tell you to look out for baby blues. Just a blip on your voyage through motherhood. It might happen at the two-week mark, and then it's happy sailing for the blessed babe. At two weeks, my mother who had come to visit from Canada, had to leave. My sister who had followed left about a week later. My husband returned to work. My life-long friends, the friends who would just turn up to do the dishes and laundry without having to be directed or asked, were all in Toronto. I was left with a baby I had not bonded with, a body that was still blue and a head that kept questioning why everyone else could do it, but I couldn't.

The prenatal classes don't prepare you for what might happen if the baby blues don't go away. Parents don't share when they became so anxious that they forget what not being anxious feels like. I never told anyone that sometimes I wanted to throw my baby against the wall or drop him from a height. I didn't say that sometimes having my baby touch me made my skin burn. I wanted to send him back. I wanted to turn back the clock to when I didn't want a baby. Parents at baby groups marvelled at their babies and the incredible capabilities of mothers. To be honest, that was my story too – when I was with them.

Then, my hormones settled and I finally found consistency. However, it was a constant state of obsessive anxiety. My baby has permanent scarring on his face from his birth. Does that mean he's brain-damaged? A series of seizures sent us to Great Ormond Street. I focused my obsession on his sleep. He must have the requisite number of hours of sleep a day or he will not develop as he should. If he didn't sleep well at night, it was because I didn't feed him properly, bathe him properly, sing to him properly, love him properly.

"Stop worrying so much about him. He's fine!" He was, but I wasn't. I focused so much on what I wasn't doing, or what I was doing wrong because the stories of those who had given birth before me were filled with mothers who were doing it right. My husband tried to tell me that I needed to get help. I said I needed to try harder.

Then the zombies came.

We lived in a ground floor flat with lovely floor to ceiling windows. The windows could not provide adequate protection in a zombie attack. Yes, it was irrational. I was a highly educated, fully functioning woman who began to see zombies at the windows. And I couldn't protect my baby. The zombies would come and I couldn't find a way out with my son. When my husband went away for work, I would devise escape plans, rather than sleep. But there was no escape. I could never get out with my baby. I tried to find places to hide in the flat. But they always found us because my son would cry. Exhausted, I finally told my husband – not because I thought it was odd that I was planning for a zombie apocalypse, but because I wanted him to help me better protect our son from the zombies.

Thanks to my husband's insistence and our incredible NHS, ten months after the birth of my son, I finally got help. Silenced stories from a traumatic childhood came out. I learned how to control my anxiety and the hallucinations gradually stopped. One in ten women experience postpartum depression, yet no one I knew shared with me their experience of it. Now, five years after the birth of my son, I tentatively share my experience, if someone asks.

With the birth of my daughter, we were better prepared. We were on watch for the signs. They came slowly, when I began to wonder what it would be like to jump off the bridge or to swerve into oncoming traffic. Or when I thought my children could be better looked after by my in-laws if I wasn't there. When I thought it would be so much better if I just didn't exist. When I thought of ways to leave life behind. This time I was more prepared to seek professional help.

What is a mother? The Korean ideal of a woman I had known was of one that was forever a young, lithe, wrinkle-free, baby-faced celebrity or a martyr-mother – one who sacrifices her career, her body, her freedom and herself for her family, her children. My own mother was a martyr-mother. She gave herself up for us. It was not what I wanted to be. But that happened. I have unwillingly given myself up to parenthood. I was woefully underprepared for what being a mother really meant. My identity as a writer, teacher, PhD researcher, wife are now inextricably inter-twined with being a mother.

As I write this, I realise I am tugging at those threads that existed before my children were born. I am attempting to regain control over my story by telling it. And at the end of a long day (or really, in the middle of an interminable morning), when small hands gently cup and pat my cheeks and a small voice says, "Chubby, chubby!" would I say that it was all worth it? Honestly, I'm still not sure. However, I can be grateful that the zombies have yet to make an encore appearance.

HUMA QURESHI

I NEVER SET OUT TO WRITE A MEMOIR

I never set out to write a memoir. The idea had rarely crossed my mind. I imagine most memoirists say the same, and I don't especially think of myself as a memoirist anyway. I never thought my life was remotely interesting enough to fill an entire book and, besides, I've always been a little shy and would ordinarily describe myself as quite private. As a former journalist, I had written occasional first-person pieces but if I am honest, I wrote them not because I always wanted to but because I knew it was a way to score an often much-needed byline, and sometimes as a freelancer, I couldn't say no to what was asked of me. But still, I had always kept certain boundaries. I told myself I would never write too closely about my marriage, my children, my family, my love life. And yet here I am, with my book, *How We Met: A Memoir of Love and Other Misadventures*, which is about all of the above and more.

I can't quite pinpoint the moment my boundaries shifted, but I think it started with a change in my reading habits. At some point in my early thirties, all I wanted was to read about real experiences about the ordinary yet astonishing challenges of life, and I found these in memoirs, mostly written by women. I pushed novels to the side and became preoccupied with reading memoirs in a hungry way, perhaps because my own life had in some ways slowed down. I had three small children, at one time all under the age of three and a half, and though daily life was in many ways chaotic, it was also very much the same every day. I didn't really know what I was going to do next with my career or my writing, or if I'd find space for it again, and sometimes the panic of this overwhelmed me. I suppose I craved stories that showed me how one could go through something immense and still come out the other side, changed or otherwise. I felt somehow less alone, no matter how far removed these stories were from the realities of my every day. Through reading the likes of Rachel Cusk, Deborah Levy and the essays of Sinead Gleeson and Emilie Pine, I felt the power and the vulnerability of writing in first person in a way I'd not felt before.

I felt, then, this urgency to capture some of the whirlwind of life happening around me and pin it down before it slipped away. I started writing notes and untitled documents and blog posts about moments of my everyday that had moved me somehow, or things I had felt or simply things my children had said, but I still never intended any of it to find its way into a book. I just wrote it for me, or sometimes the small handful of people who occasionally read my then-outdated blog. I wrote an article for *The Guardian* sharing my love of memoirs and an editor from a publisher happened to read it and sent me a DM over Twitter, asking if I had any of my own material to share.

I'll admit, I was wary and didn't immediately reply. Though writing was all I'd ever wanted to do, my confidence was at an all-time low and I'd got my hopes up too many times before only to be deeply disappointed. Several months earlier, before *The Guardian* article, I'd had a collection of essays about love, loss and loneliness out on submission and every large publisher had rejected it. Though they all agreed it was beautifully written, they found it 'too quiet', not loud enough. I took the criticism badly. I convinced myself that in being too quiet, my writing was therefore meaningless. I convinced myself that it didn't deserve space, that *I* didn't deserve space, and that my stories weren't loud enough to be worth telling.

And yet, the DM in my inbox sat there, and one thing led to another and so in the end, I shared with that editor, whose name was Olivia, some of the untitled pieces I'd written. One of them described how I met my husband, who happened to be English, and how he was not exactly what my fairly conservative, south Asian family expected. 'This is good,' she said, 'But I think you can go deeper. I think you need to ask yourself what the real story is here.'

She wanted me to go deeper, but not necessarily louder. And that made sense to me. And I appreciated her not pointing a remote control at my writing, telling me to put the volume up. After speaking with Olivia, I went away and read *The Situation and The Story: The Art of Personal Narrative* by Vivian Gornick (which I'd recommend to anyone interested in narrative nonfiction) and after writing the question "What's my story really about?" repeatedly in a notebook, I sat down and wrote what was to become the opening of *How We Met*. The more I wrote, the more *How We Met*'s existence began to feel necessary to me. Though so many of the memoirs I had read spoke to me, I was aware that most were by white writers and very few reflected the stories of women like me, who shared my background or were brought up in a world like mine, and I realised how much I had desperately missed that. I wondered if my story might count for something. I began to wonder whether perhaps there was a kind of strength in quiet writing after all.

Perhaps that's when I fully let go of those boundaries I'd put upon myself, and gave myself permission to write openly from a place of deep honesty. I wrote the first draft furiously between Christmas 2019 and February 2020 and sent it to Olivia. I signed my book deal for *How We Met* not long after.

How We Met looks and sounds like a love story, because the premise is about how I met my husband, of whom my family didn't at first approve, and how I navigated that path with them and him, but it's also so much more than that. In writing *How We Met*, I came face to face with my younger self, who was lost and oftentimes bewildered and out of her depth, and I wanted, in a way, to write for her, so that she might know that in the end, things turned out okay. I also write fiction, with my collection of short stories, *Things We Do Not Tell The People We Love,* published in 2021 and my novel, *Playing Games,* in 2023; my stories take me to unspoken places of sadness and often, though not always, end in tragedy. But *How We Met* is not like that, and it mattered to me to write myself a happy ending with a resolution that felt complete. I thought often of my children as I wrote my memoir, and I hope that one day they might read it and know what it means, to be a family, to grow up, to make mistakes; to love and be loved.

Even now, with four books to my name, I still think about those early rejections, the ones that told me that I was too quiet and not nearly noisy enough. I wonder sometimes if what they really meant was – my story didn't fit the narrative they wanted from me, as a woman of a certain background. Looking back, it seems like such a gendered comment to make; would a man's words ever be considered in the same way? And so this is why it matters to me all the more to write my own story, in my own voice, and not have it assumed for me by somebody else. These days, I remind myself that perhaps there is something meaningful in not demanding to be heard, but instead simply inviting a reader to come take a seat, to sit opposite me; to listen to what I have to say instead of me blindly shouting it. To me, there is something quietly empowering in this simple act.

MINOLI SALGADO

THE FAREWELL PARTY

'History is natural selection,' Salman Rushdie has claimed. Some stories struggle into daylight; others fade away, leaving only silent artefacts behind.

What, though, of the stories that are not quite lost to us, those that continue to circulate but are threatened with extinction? Stories that are unheard not because no one hears them but because no one takes the trouble to listen and respond? These stories - narratives on the edge of remembrance – abound. And these are the narratives that galvanize many of us to write.

The narratives that emerged from Sri Lanka, my ancestral home, during and after the civil war, have taken many forms. Novels and short stories abound and most moving, perhaps, and least known are poems written in Tamil, the language spoken by the main minority group who were the primary targets of the war. Much literature on the war is published – indeed self-published – in the country and in local languages. Much of this work endorses the official political narrative on the war as an act of liberation by the state. The few literary books that are published abroad usually challenge this official story and some might, just might, be heard and reviewed, listened to, and generate debate.

There are thousands more narratives, real stories of war, that lie on the cusp of the historical record, on the edge of inscription and memory. These narratives remain as unfinished and unresolved as the trauma they reflect. Many of these narratives embrace the experiences of relatives of the disappeared whose mission is to find out what happened to their lost loved ones. The war generated tens of thousands of enforced disappearances carried out mainly by the state and paramilitaries, disappearances recognised internationally as a statistical fact. But very, very few of the narratives on disappearance have made it into the light of publication; even fewer have been personalised and given a human face.

In 2018, I returned to Sri Lanka and travelled round the country speaking to victim-survivors of war who had appealed – in vain – to national and international organisations for redress. They came carrying sheafs of documents, along with birth certificates and photographs of lost loved ones that gave proof that they had lived. I spent hours in darkened rooms listening to their stories, recording memories that evolved into a book. It became a kind of travelling memorialisation marked by the milestones of their memories as I moved across the land.

And in April 2022, I returned again and joined a public protest that was making the headlines in its call for the president to step down. A serious economic crisis, the worst in the country's history, had led to the country defaulting on a $51 billion debt and the president and his family were held responsible. The crisis resulted in fuel queues that snaked through streets blocking the roads of the capital, Colombo. There were daily power cuts, medical shortages and eleven-hour water-cuts. People died of heat exhaustion while waiting to get petrol and gas.

The protests had come together earlier that month at the seafront at Galle Face, a mile-long stretch of green that fronts the Presidential secretariat. A tented village, called GotaGoGama, or 'Gota Go Village', grew spontaneously here. In a country where essentials had dried up, the site distributed free food, free water, free medical aid, free legal aid, free battery charging facilities and free public lectures by local and international academics. It hosted open mic forums, a lending library, musical performances by up to 2000 artistes, street theatre, art shows, all of them held under banners of black and white that called in loud letters, 'Gota Go Home', 'Give Our Stolen Money Back'. The protests continued for several weeks and went on through the night, in the dark absence of street lights and windy gusts of monsoon rain.

The protests attracted global attention: first as an exemplar of peaceful resistance and later for the arson and mass arrests that followed a politically-sanctioned riot that broke them up. The protests were successful. Gota did 'go home' along with his brother, the Prime Minister, but the voices they drew together – voices that united communities as never before – have since been suppressed.

I spent some weeks at GotaGoGama and it was here that I met Jennifer Weerasinghe sitting in a white tent that was covered with signs that called for justice in all three official languages. She was sitting quietly with her husband and a friend in a space occupied exclusively by relatives of the disappeared. Jennifer told me she had taken the case of her disappeared son to the press many times but that this was the first time she felt she had been heard. Above the din of electricity generators, she said she had never been able to talk about the abduction in such a large space. Even the media who took down her story did not always report it because they were not allowed. 'When I came here,' she explained, 'I felt empowered especially when I saw the youth of the country speak up. I felt young again and met a lot of the families of the disappeared from Jaffna [the region mainly populated by Tamils], too.'

She then gave me details of the last time she saw her son, Dilan Jamaldeen, who was 23 when he was disappeared in 2008. He had gone with four other young men to a friend's farewell party in town. The friend, Rajiv Naganathan, was heading to study medicine in the UK. Dilan was disappeared with Rajiv and the others and she knows one of those responsible for the abduction: Rajiv's vehicle was found with false number plates in the possession of a now-retired captain in the Navy. The captain had gifted it to his wife for her birthday, Jennifer said. The captain retired with full military honours in 2021.

Dilan's abduction was part of a series of kidnappings carried out by Navy personnel for ransom, a case known as the 'Navy 11' that is unique in the country's history for being the first in which witnesses and accused were both from the naval corps. The story made it into Amnesty International files but remains unresolved as successive political leaders have worked to protect the accused.

Jennifer gave the name of the man with the stolen car. Her husband repeated this to be sure I noted it down. The judder of the generator and incessant cries of protestors made it difficult to hear her, but the name came clear and strong. Jennifer and her husband want justice. Her husband, a retired armed officer, 'a war hero', expects to be well served by the country he had served.

The civil war had ended brutally in May 2009 after the

intensification of a military conflict led by Gotabaya Rajapakse who was defence secretary at the time. Gotabaya's time in office saw a steep rise in enforced disappearances. His response to the urgent call for answers from the families of the disappeared was dismissive and damning: he told them that their missing ones were 'actually dead'.

Jennifer relentlessly pursued her quest for her missing son, for answers and for justice, pursued these through the courts, international agencies and the media for fourteen long years. Now here at the protest site, she was emboldened and had renewed faith: 'When I see this younger generation, I feel strong. We will win, our cases will come out some day. I believe my child is out there alive, there are a lot of reasons they are not giving him back. But the people from Jaffna don't know anything about what happened to their children. When my child comes out, this government will have to provide answers as to what happened to those children as well.'

And she continued to call out wrongs and mark the importance of being heard. 'How many people are going through things like this? There are many people who are scared to speak out. I used to feel afraid but I am without fear now. We speak out, letting our blood boil, while our throats turn dry. The government has to listen. Through speaking out like this, I can tell the whole world.'

Jennifer's story is one of many that rest on the cusp of history, a story half-heard, a story that struggles to reach the international fora that she said are the only place where a productive intervention might be made. I am conscious that a story of two farewell parties – her son's friend's party and the protest itself that led to the president's resignation – might dissolve into a murmur in the surge of events.

Yet I am also conscious that, like all half-heard stories, Jennifer's story pulses with life. It is an open question, a sleeping giant that only needs a shift in the weather to rouse it to roar. Recently the US blacklisted a key accused in the Navy 11 case, Captain Karannagoda, who was then promptly fired from a governorship by the current president who wished to distance himself from him. An international audience does indeed make a difference, as Jennifer pointed out.

These half-heard stories call us into awareness; they occupy the space between listening and response. They close the distance between peoples and cultures, create new communities of belonging, and compel us to activate the freedoms that make words work. To write them is humbling and a huge privilege. To hear them is a necessity if we wish to become whole.

YVONNE SINGH

THE STORY OF A REAL 'LONELY LONDONER'

On a clear November night in 1961, as the sky darkened and netted with stars, my father remembers leaving a balmy Trinidad aboard the *SS Ascania*, watching from the deck as the island's rainbow-coloured lights receded into the distance. Three months later, he arrived in a frosty Southampton in the brutal and unforgiving winter of January 1962. (The boat's propeller had broken down and a two-week journey had taken three months via Martinique and Funchal, Madeira, a Portuguese island.)

It was -4C and he remembers his fingers sticking to the metal guardrail on deck.

"It was extraordinary cold, like the inside of a freezer. Your breath misting and making shapes. When we disembark, people were so cold, they were covering their faces with towels and using anything they had to wrap around their heads to ward off the chill. We had no scarf. One elderly West Indian lady was walking around cussing us. 'Take that off your ears,' she was saying. 'They will photograph you and it will appear in Trinidad and Guyana about how y'all behave.'"

The press attention to the new arrivals was largely hostile. Articles describing "the flood of migrants", threatening scarce housing and jobs, were common. At the time my father was arriving, the mood in Britain had shifted against the "open door policy" of the 1948 Nationality Act, which had heralded the arrival of the *HMT Empire Windrush* and a large wave of migration from Britain's colonies in the Caribbean. Many of those who travelled were citizens of the UK and colonies, held British passports and equal rights of residence. But as numbers grew, from 46,850 in 1956 to 140,000 in 1961, the reception that greeted them became less friendly.

Ugly race riots had erupted in London's Notting Hill and Robin Hood Chase in Nottingham in 1958, and in 1960 an increasingly jittery Conservative government sought to restrict entry. The same month my father departed Trinidad, a Commonwealth Immigrants Bill had started making its way through the House of Commons, becoming law on 1 July 1962, and ending the automatic right of people in the British Commonwealth and Colonies to settle in the UK.

On disembarking the boat, my father, wrapped in the woollen herringbone coat he had purchased in Spain, tried desperately to stop the wind slicing through his thin seersucker trousers as he clutched his cardboard grip tightly. Nestled inside it, among a change of clothes, were the dregs of a bottle of El Dorado rum that he had purchased to celebrate his 21st birthday on board ship, and three prized secondhand Newton textbooks in Maths, Physics and Applied Maths, their spines cracked and broken after years of use.

He had travelled 4,000 miles from the small village of Maria's Pleasure in Essequibo, in then British Guiana to study and work in England. There were rumours of plenty of job opportunities, and his dream was to be an engineer.

There were no universities in Guyana, and the US had clamped down on immigration from the Caribbean with the 1952 McCarran-Walter Act, and my father, the eldest of ten children, rejected the notion of backbreaking work on the family farm.

"I was very stubborn. I had my own ideas of what I wanted to be. I wanted to support myself," he says. "I knew with an English education, I would be accepted anywhere in the world."

In his pocket he had a scrap of paper scrawled with the name of his friend, Winston Bacchus, in Ladbroke Grove. He had no idea where Ladbroke Grove was. All he knew was that it was somewhere in London. "I had no clue about life outside Georgetown," my dad admits wryly.

His parents had reassured him that if he was unhappy, all he needed to do was write and they would somehow find the $2,000 US fare to bring him home. In that first year, my father composed a letter three times on that thin, transparent blue airmail paper familiar to so many West Indians.

Every time the letter remained crumpled in his pocket, crushed like moths' wings.

At Southampton, my father cut a forlorn figure as bodies milled around him intent on getting to their destinations. All he had on him was a £28 traveller's cheque and nowhere to cash it. A young Trinidadian nurse took pity on him and loaned him the money to get to Waterloo.

At the station, two acquaintances from the same district in Guyana, John and Simon, were there to meet him (to this day, he has no idea how they knew when he was arriving; the boat had been delayed after all). His friends had arranged accommodation for him for a few days in Lawford Road in Kentish Town while he found his feet. He remembers being bundled in a cab and an address being shouted at the driver.

As my father stared out of the cab window, he could see huddled figures shovelling snow off the roads just so that cars would pass. "There were four-foot drifts on the streets of Kentish Town".

It felt like the world he had arrived in had had all the colour drained out of it: the sky, a dishwater grey; the landscape, a ghostly white – "like someone had taken a pack of flour and buss it open, covering houses, trees and everything. It was the first time I had seen snow."

The Victorian house in Lawford Road had been divided into a labyrinthine series of rooms, all of which were rented out. My father stayed in a "fellow named Bob's room", and he recalls four new arrivals huddling around a two-bar electric fire while a blizzard wailed outside the battered sash windows.

At the house, he met a good friend from back home, William from Wakenham, known as "Boy" on account of his cheeky personality. Boy was ten years older and had been in London for two years. He had a job as a cleaner at the British Museum, and seemed savvy about big city life. He convinced my father to leave the cramped premises of Lawford Road after a few days and get a paying room in Campdell Road. "We can sweet-talk the landlady," he urged my dad. "And get cheaper rent."

My dad obliged, but four weeks after Boy and he found a place, Boy changed his mind – he had been dating an English girl named Ann for about 12 months and he had decided to move in with her. My father couldn't afford the room on his own and found himself on the streets – homeless and jobless, with just £26 left of the traveller's cheque. Those days, he believes, were his most anxious in London. My father's first point of call was the noticeboard at Tufnell Park Station, where accommodation and jobs were regularly advertised, but underneath the script, advertising rooms to rent, were written the words: "No blacks, no dogs, no Irish."

"You would turn up with your cash in your hand and they would say: 'Sorry, the room has gone.' But the advert would be in the station the next day."

That night my father wore shoe leather, pounding the streets looking for vacancy signs. Again the kindness of strangers helped him. A West African family took him in to their home at 7pm at night and allowed him to stay in the cupboard under the stairs.

The next day he started again on his search. It was then that the loneliness of the big city crushed him. "We were so lonely when we arrived. We didn't have family and friends. This was a place where we didn't go to school or university, there were no networks around us," he says.

His luck eventually changed and he got a room at 78 Patshull Road in Kentish Town for £3 a week, with a kind Polish landlady.

Here, he also found work as a warehouseman for a family firm called Harrison that supplied baths, sinks and toilets for the council and was paid £10 a week. The work was hard, physical labour. He noted he had to remain in the back room, lifting and loading lead pipes on a pulley to prepare the orders, and he was never allowed at the front of the shop. After finding work, life became better for my father. He became good friends with an Anglo-Indian boy called Richard, who lived in the next room, and worked for a scientific instruments firm. "He thought he was Elvis

Presley, always combing his hair backwards and dancing around the mirror." Boy and Ann also bounced back into his life.

Richard tried to get him a clerical job, as he could see how worn out my father was working at Harrison. Ann even took him to Mount Pleasant Post Office to sit a clerical exam to get work as a postman. "I must have applied for 300 jobs," he says.

When the cost of a can of spilled paint was docked out of his wages at Harrison, my father's search for labour intensified. He got a job as a van assistant on school meals delivery. Here the work was easier and he was paid well, £13 a week. His manager, Mrs Abbott, an English lady, treated him "like a son" and would cook him full English breakfasts. At work he met Big Derek, a Trinidadian, whose friends shared rooms in a large house in Caversham Road in Kentish Town. Derek loved music and the walls of his room were lined with records: "All the jazz greats: Nat King Cole, Satchmo, Brook Benton".

Derek and his flatmates would host open house at weekends. According to my dad, "Everyone would go there, not just West Indians, English people as well who work in Woolworths and Marks & Spencer, and anyone who found the dress codes and expense of the West End nightclubs too much would come there and lime in the afternoon."

It took two years for my father to settle into life in the UK, and he recalls those early days as "mental, a story of survival, always striving to get rent and food."

His is a story of a real lonely Londoner, embodying the struggles of a generation of West Indians, who arrived in the UK post-war. This year marked the 75th anniversary of the arrival of the *Empire Windrush*. As that generation is slowly lost to us, their stories matter now more than ever.

MAHSUDA SNAITH

THE VERSIONS OF ME YOU DO NOT SEE

I visited a hall of mirrors once. I hadn't meant to; I'd gone to an aquarium and the hall of mirrors was tagged onto the end without any signs indicating how to get out. At first it was disorientating seeing so many versions of myself. There I was right in front of me and next to me and behind me. There I was refracted a thousand times over into smaller versions of myself. From the corner of my eye, I saw another person with their back towards me. Then I saw another person in the same clothes. It took a while for me to figure out that, on this midweek morning during term time, I was the only person in the room. Every image I saw was, in fact, another version of myself. It was a relief to realise this but also refreshing to see myself from a new angle.

There are many versions of us, depending on the day, the mood, the refraction of light. Yet sometimes it takes a while for people to see past the image they think we should be. This is particularly the case when you're a woman, more so when you're a woman of colour and even more so when you're a *creative* woman of colour. Not a doctor or a pharmacist? You're a writer you say? How do your parents feel about that? I've had the latter question asked in a number of author interviews. White writers may get asked this question too, but usually after they've discussed having a fraught relationship with their parents. When you're a South Asian woman, the fraught relationship is assumed.

I've had assumptions made about me all my life. Going to Indian restaurants I am asked which are the best dishes on the menu even when I've never been to that restaurant before. People expected me to spend summers at large, Asian weddings dancing to Bollywood songs with my large, Asian family. We were Bangladeshi-Muslim, so there was neither Bollywood nor dancing in our household, and my mother had left my father when we were children, which led to us being cut off from most of our extended family. We were on our own, just the five of us, the only South Asian family on our predominately white council estate. There was no ready stereotype for us.

The 8-year-old version of myself was completely naïve about the version people thought she should be. Sitting in primary school she learnt, with crossed legs and wide eyes, that being a writer was a *job* and that you could do it for *a living*. Suddenly she knew exactly what she wanted to be and didn't think being British-Bangladeshi, or a girl, or from a single-parent family living on a council estate in Leicester would in any way stop her.

The 13-year-old version of myself was still striving to be a writer. Shy and awkward, she would hide in the school library during lunchtimes because it was the one place she felt truly safe. This version read all the books she could find, then wrote thinly veiled attempts at 'Point Horror' and 'Anne of Green Gables' books. This version would enter writing competitions for adults with no thought about whether she was ready to be sending *any* work out yet. This version had not yet noticed that none of the books on those library shelves had people who looked like her in them, let alone were written by people who looked like her. Later, when she started seeking out books by South Asian writers, she would find books with starkly similar themes; usually sari print on the cover and a mention of bhajis in the blurb. It was as if the publishing industry could only see one version of us too.

My 16-year-old-self still had the conviction she could be a writer and decided it was time she wrote an *original* novel. But, as she hadn't ever travelled any further than Blackpool for the day, she couldn't think of any other settings than the Leicester council estate she'd been brought up in (at least she wouldn't have to do much research). This version wrote the novel in a thick note-book she'd been given as a gift. She did not plan the story but let it take its own course, centring around a British-Bangladeshi character and childhood friendship, other areas that did not require research.

There is another version of this 16-year-old-self, the one who believed she wasn't writing about her own life, who believed she wrote to escape the world and walk in someone else's shoes. Which she did too, in her own way. But what this version didn't realise was that, when she wrote this story, she was actually looking at an image of herself.

This 16-year-old-self wrote about playing in small patches of urban woodland with her friends, of mothers who visited their GPs on a regular basis, whether they needed it or not. She wrote about boys who sat on bikes terrorising the neighbourhood and a child who under-stood the language her mother spoke but was barely able to speak a word of this language herself (to this day, my older self has elderly South Asian women speaking to me in a range of languages and looking downright disappointed when they realise I can't speak any). This self wrote about larger-than-life characters. Of the stories children create when they aren't told the truth by the adults around them. Of love. Of grief. In short, she wrote about the world she knew about. She wasn't trying to be ground-breaking by focusing on people and places rarely seen in mainstream publishing, she was writing about the only thing she could at the time.

I wonder, if that version of myself had known how hard it would be to get this story out in the world, how she would have felt. Because it was hard. After working on a couple of (failed) novels, it wasn't until I was nearing my 30s that I came back to that thick notebook with the story of a British-Bangladeshi girl growing up on council estate within it. I read it and cringed but decided that, although there was much to work on, I still loved the characters and setting. I rewrote the novel from scratch, using all the writing skills I'd learnt through those failed novels to create a new version (even novels have many versions of themselves). I joined writers' clubs, applied for various development opportunities and kept on working on my writing until I felt my manuscript was strong enough to submit to agents. Then I submitted.

Tumbleweed.

I received no rejection slips or emails, no responses at all. I didn't know what I was doing wrong, or even what I was doing right. At times, that early-30s version of myself thought about giving up completely; it was time for me to forget those unrealistic dreams. I'd seen the evidence on the shelves; people like me didn't become writers. But I still had this voice inside me, my 8-year-old-self perhaps, who told me I could do this. So, I began submitting my novel to competitions.

I won the SI Leeds Prize on my 35th birthday. This version of myself had been relieved to be shortlisted and amazed to have won. The judges had seen potential in a book I was starting to doubt would see the light of day. Suddenly, I had hope that my novel had legs. And it had. When *The Things We Thought We Knew* was published, I was named an *Observer New Face of Fiction* and it later became a *World Book Night Book*. One agent, an editor and two books later, my current 41-year-old-self has spoken at book events and festivals, judged prizes, lead creative writing workshops and is now a mentor to other writers. It was in no way easy, and I have continuously clashed with people's version of what they think I should be. The micro-aggressions at panel events, assumptions about my characters based on nothing other than their skin colour, the 'How do your parents feel about you being a writer?' question. I recently performed at a local event and was telling someone about my debut novel.

"So where did you grow up?" they asked. "Not on a council estate? Ha!"

The laugh was the killer; filled with an assumption that I couldn't possibly come from such a background. When I told them I did, the person quickly moved the conversation forward.

We all make incorrect assumptions; we're human, we mess up. For me, the worst thing is when people refuse to look at the version in front of them. The image that gives a different perspective. But we aren't responsible for what people assume about us. All we're responsible for is living our own complex, multi-layered lives, in the way that feels true to us. And, if we feel the urge, to write about this with every version of ourselves welcomed.

SHEREEN TADROS

I THOUGHT IT WAS YOU

No-one ever tells me I look like my mother. They examine the photos I have on display, staring into her celluloid eyes. There's the one where she is standing in the balcony of my parents' old flat in Cairo, looking into the middle distance with an impossibly serene expression on her face and my toddler siblings implausibly groomed as they hold onto her skirt. Or the one where she is two decades older, on a beach, wavy hair blowing in the breeze, not a scrap of make-up, laughing and looking slightly wild. People pause over these photographs and eventually say, "Wow, your mother is really beautiful." Without a hint of irony, they almost invariably follow it up with, "You look nothing like her."

I sometimes wonder if that is my punishment. Because although my mother was elegant, educated, kind and, yes, certainly beautiful, I am haunted that I once willed her not to be mine.

It was the last day of Year 5. At morning break, I held out a tray of cakes at the door of my classroom. With a birthday in the middle of the summer holidays, I hadn't wanted to miss out on the ritual of serving sweets to my classmates.

My mother had made the cakes with me the night

before, showing me how to mix the glacé icing to the right consistency. I had longed to use a packet mix with rice paper decorations of the Flintstones, but my mother had looked at the ingredients and put them back on the shelf. We compromised with a jar of sugared cherries and the cakes were neater, more perfect than any that had been served that year.

Nina, the most popular girl in my class, who had freckles and who always had crisps in her lunchbox, was first in line. Taking a cake, she peeled off the cherry with her teeth. She spread her arms wide, and, in a falsely operatic tone, sang 'Happy Birthday.' It started off beautifully. It ended with her comparing me to a shit.

"...*And I thought it was you.*" She held the last note, bits of jellied cherry stuck to her front incisors, red and luscious.

I smiled uncertainly. No big deal. Sure, it was a bit more extreme than the *monkey in the zoo* variation that people sang. But it was only a joke.

"Because you're brown!" Nina explained, delighted.

There was a moment of general agreement, a few 'oh yeah's' rippling through the line. And then, everyone laughed.

Even my best friend, Ella, whose secrets I had kept since we were three (to this day, I've told no one that she once had an accident on the way to the bathroom and shat in my mother's slipper).

Even James, with whom I wrote and performed plays, and who blushed when our arms brushed.

Even Ruth, whose parents took me to Sunday School and who was known as the kindest girl in our class.

Everyone.

I tried to laugh with them but I could feel my face

flushing, tears hot and heavy in my eyes.

"Well, don't cry about it," Nina said. "It's just a joke. Because you're brown," she repeated, gesturing in my general vicinity. "It's funny."

Afterwards, Ella trailed behind me, trying to convince me Nina hadn't meant anything by it. "And… well, you *are* brown, aren't you?"

My teacher, Miss Morley, didn't seem to have noticed. But later, handing me back my exercise book, she quietly told me the best thing to do was just to ignore such behaviour, particularly since 'in ten years' time, you will have forgotten all about Nina and she will be working at Wimpy.' (Side note: Nina apparently now runs a successful estate agency).

That evening, I examined myself in the mirror. I knew I was different to my schoolmates. I knew that new people called me 'Charlene' instead of Shereen because *Neighbours* was big then and *Shereen* was just too tricky. I knew that when I proudly told people I was a descendent of one of the oldest civilisations in the world, they invariably *walked like an Egyptian*. But I had never thought I looked like shit. Specifically, *the colour of shit*. I pulled at the skin of my cheeks. How many shades would it take to be closer to human flesh than excrement?

At dinner, I was uninterested in the okra my mother had cooked. She felt my forehead with the back of her hand. "Not warm. *Malik*?" she asked.

"I hate okra." I said. "Why does it have to be so slimy?"

"It's God's provision," my mother said. "Don't be ungrateful."

"It's disgusting," I said.

My mother gave me her special look: the smallest inclination of the eyes towards you that nonetheless made you want to be absorbed into the earth rather than have disappointed her.

My sister kicked me under the table but it was too late.

"Why can't we have chips?"

"We have chips all the time!" my sister said, trying, frantically, to shut me up.

"Not like everyone else. Do you remember when Lisa came over and asked for chips and instead of just giving us oven chips with ketchup, Mama peeled them and chopped them and fried them and served them with a pinch bowl of *cumin on the table*? I thought I would die of embarrassment." (What I didn't say was that Lisa, even after having been served the vinegar she had requested, and even had seconds, had told everyone that the cumin smelled like B.O.).

My mother said nothing but rose to wash her bowl.

"And why do I have to have pitta bread in my lunch box? No one else has olives or mortadella in their sandwiches."

"You love olives," my sister said. "And she goes across town to the deli especially for your mortadella."

"Ella has cheese and marmite on sliced bread. *White* bread."

At this, my mother turned off the tap and turned to face me.

"*Hadir*. If that's what you want, you can have school dinners from now on. So I don't embarrass you any more."

Ouch.

Starting junior school, imagining Enid Blyton-style spreads, I had made my mother sign me up for school dinners.

That first day, the canteen was thick with the dank smell

of offal. Presented with a brown slop they told me was liver and bacon, I gagged trying to force it down, the lunch monitors invoking starving children in Ethiopia.

When I related my ordeal, my mother had been torn between mirth and horror. Despite having already paid for a whole term of 'dinners,' she had made me a packed lunch every day since.

That was when I said it, the words cold and deliberate in my mouth.

"I wish Ella's mum was my mum."

My mother's eyes widened for a moment, and she swept away to the living room, where she played an Oum Kalsoum record and attacked a needlepoint she had been trying to complete for the past eighteen months. She only picked it up when she was angry. I could see her through the hatch from the kitchen as my sister and I whispered.

"What did you say that for?" my sister hissed.

"I *do* wish that!"

"How can you?" My sister's friends, who had the benefit of being older and wiser, swooned over my mother. Her divine accent. Her huge eyes. The fresh mint she grew in the garden to serve in tea. *How chic!*

"I just want to be the same as everyone else."

My mother, the other side of the hatch, got up and closed its doors. Oum Kalsoum's song of lost love muffling, still, through them.

My sister shook her head. "You're crazy. You don't know anything about anything."

The worst of it was that I did.

I knew my mother, who had graduated top of her class, was one of only six women in her year at medical school in Alexandria. I knew she was infuriated by the other five, who said they were too delicate to do dissection and gave their turns with the scalpel to the men. I knew that as a Copt, she was in a double minority, and was made to recite large sections of the Quran as part of her final year anatomy exams. I knew she chose a career in paediatrics because, (an unfashionable answer, but the truth) she adored children. I knew that, under Sadat's military regime, soldiers rose and saluted her as *'Captain Doctora.'* I knew that when she came to the UK, following my father's career, their first home was in a street of lodging houses with proud signs in the downstairs windows reading, 'No Blacks, No Irish.' I knew that here, her experience counted for nothing, and she had to prove her knowledge in exam after paid exam. I knew - because I figured it out, and resolutely not because she ever gave me any inkling - that I had been a surprise third child, born in a country where she had no family, no support structure, no hospital crèche. I knew, from my father, that when she was branded a *geriatric multip* at the age of 37, that she had declined an amniocentesis on the basis that she would do nothing differently. I knew that when I was born, she cried that her parents, recently deceased, would not meet me this side of heaven. I knew that at the end of a miserable week when she was working two counties away; when the babysitter did not show up and my father, an obstetrician, had to hold the fort; when everything was chaotic and awful, she had finally handed in her notice.

I knew that she had given up career and status and all those years of work and study for me, her unplanned child.

I knew, because she told me often, that I was, variously, her heart, her soul, her eyes. I knew that her every move towards me was love.

And yet, more than anything, I still wanted, and wanted her, to be like everyone else.

To speak English with a Home Counties accent; to go on holidays to Norfolk; to have nothing more exotic than creamed rice in the pantry; and most of all, to be white.

Later that night, filled with remorse, I threw myself on her lap and told her I never wanted any mother but her.

And she, being my mother, stroked my hair, called me her beloved, and forgave me.

Some years later, when I was eighteen, my mother lay in bed quizzing me on the branches of the cardiac arteries. Her voice tight with pain, she had refused morphine in order to be fully present with us kids.

I was in my first year of medical school. When my father, famously stoic, had called me the week before my end of year exams to gently suggest I might want to consider visiting, I knew I had to rush home. My mother, who had non-Hodgkins lymphoma, had been admitted to hospital.

Her prognosis was meant to be good but I guess she had never quite done what was expected.

One evening, while my siblings and I sat with her, she was in so much pain, we begged her to take the offered opioids. She eventually agreed, but, worried that the drugs would take her words away, she first told us each how much she loved us. Carefully, so as not to shear her damaged skin, I held her hand. "I'm so glad you are my mother," I told her.

Many years after she died (in the house I shared with the husband my mother had predicted I would marry), my father asked me to pass him a framed photograph from the mantelpiece. It was my mother, in an unknown garden, smiling broadly.

He raised his glasses to peer at it. "Do you know," he told me, "I thought that was you."

AUTHOR BIOGRAPHIES

Yasmin Alibhai Brown is a journalist, broadcaster and author. She writes for the i newspaper and has written for the *Guardian*, *Observer*, *Sunday Times*, *Mail on Sunday*, *Daily Mail*, *Time Magazine* and others. Her awards include the Orwell Prize for Political Writing and National Press Awards Columnist of the Year. She is a part-time professor of journalism at Middlesex University. She is co- founder of the charity British Muslims for Secular Democracy. Her recent books include *Refusing the Veil*; *Exotic England*; I*n Defence of Political Correctness*; and *Ladies Who Punch*.

Kavita Bhanot published the influential essay 'Decolonise not Diversify' in 2015. She has edited four collections of short stories and essays and translated a collection of short stories from Hindi. She completed a Leverhulme Research Fellowship at Leicester University (where she remains an Honorary Fellow), a Post-Doctoral Fellowship at Ashoka University in Delhi and a Phd in Creative Writing and Literature at Manchester University. For the last twelve years, she has been a reader and mentor with The Literary Consultancy, with whom she has co-devised and co-delivers workshops on Ethical Editing. In 2023 Kavita founded and directed Jaag: Panjabi and Pahari-Pothwari Language and Literature Festival in Handsworth, Birmingham as well as the Literature Must Fall Festival and Collective. She is currently writing a book for Pluto developing her work on Literature Must Fall.

Lynne E. Blackwood is a disabled author and avid performer of poetry, short stories and novels, previously supported by the Arts Council, a mentee on The Literary Consultancy Chapter & Verse scheme and on the INSCRIBE national programme to complete a poetry chapbook. She completed a short story collection based on her Anglo-Parsi Indian family history, "A Scattering of Blue Moons", which was longlisted for the SI Leeds Prize and is currently working on transforming the collection into a series of historical novels. She also continues writing memoir "vignettes" about her eventful and colourful life, which she wishes to eventually collate into a book. Despite physical limitations and lack of 'visibility' on the literary scene, Lynne continues to strive and work hard to be represented as an author in her own right.

Gail Bolland is one of five sisters brought up on a farm near Wolverhampton. She studied Fine Art at Middlesex University and has enjoyed a varied career in the arts, which has included group exhibitions, teaching, community arts and arts in hospitals.With the Leeds Teaching Hospitals NHS Trust, she initiated and coordinated Tonic, a multi-arts project across six acute hospital sites, which partnered with other arts organisations regionally and nationally and won many Arts Council awards, including major Lottery awards. Since retiring, she has become more involved with literature. With Soroptomist International at Leeds, she was one of the co-founders and steering group members of the SI Leeds Literary Prize. She has written a well-praised who-dunnit, *A Man's Dying*, published by Zois Books and has poems in published anthologies. She is currently working on two new crime novels.

Fiona Goh is the Prize Director for the SI Leeds Literary Prize and has worked for the Prize since its inception. Based in

Yorkshire, she is a freelance arts consultant who works with organisations of all sizes across the UK and Europe to help them develop, with a particular emphasis on festivals, literature and networks. Previous clients include Holmfirth Arts Festival, Europe Jazz Network, Association of Irish Festival Events, Ilkley Literature Festival, Making Music and Out of Many Lit Fest. She is also Director of the British Arts Festivals Association and is passionate about the importance of the arts in creating vibrant and healthy communities. When not working, she can be found reading, watching films, enjoying competitive family games or trying to improve her tennis.

Kavita A. Jindal is a fiction writer, poet and essayist. Her novel, *Manual For A Decent Life*, won the Eastern Eye Award for Literature 2020, and was shortlisted for the Rabindranath Tagore Literary Prize 2021-22. She has published three slim volumes of poetry: *Raincheck Accepted*, *Raincheck Renewed* and *Patina*. Her work has appeared in anthologies and literary journals worldwide and been broadcast on BBC Radio 4, Zee TV UK and European radio stations. Selected poems have been translated into Arabic, German, Italian, Spanish, Romanian, Ukrainian and Punjabi. She previously served as Senior Editor at *Asia Literary Review* and is the co-founder of 'The Whole Kahani' collective for British Asian writers. Kavita has participated in literary festivals in the UK, US, Europe, India, and Southeast Asia. She enjoys collaborating with musicians and artists across a range of projects. www.kavitajindal.com

Suad Kamardeen is a British-Nigerian Muslim writer, editor and photographer. She is a Founding Editor of *WAYF* Journal and the Managing Editor of *Rowayat*. She is also a Creative Writing Masters student at the University of Oxford. Her young adult novel won the SI Leeds Literary Prize 2022

and her adult novel was shortlisted for Stylist Prize for Feminist Fiction 2021. Suad runs Qalb Writers Collective, a community to support Black and Muslim women writers with knowledge and resources. Suad is committed to bearing witness to the lives, histories and cultures of Black and Muslim women. Her work explores themes of intersectional identities, shame, belonging, family, female friendships and love. Connect with her at suadkamardeen.com, and @suadkamardeen across social media.

Sumana Khan is a Bengaluru-born writer and accidental data analyst living in Reading, Berkshire. Her unpublished crime novel "The Good Twin" bagged the third place as well as the Readers' Choice award in the SI Leeds Literary Prize (2020). Her short stories have been published in the *Writing Magazine* and have been longlisted/shortlisted/highly commended in various competitions such as: 2023 Bath Short Story Award; 2019 Royal Society of Literature's VS Pritchett short story competition; 2016 Just Write competition; 2016 Manchester Short Story competition. She has a MLitt in Creative Writing and a PhD in Psychology.

Winnie M. Li is an author and activist. Her debut novel *Dark Chapter* won 2nd place in the SI Leeds Literary Prize 2016, and later won The Guardian's Not The Booker Prize, was nominated for an Edgar Award, and translated into ten languages. She is currently adapting it for the screen. Her second novel *Complicit* was a New York Times' Editors' Choice, shortlisted for the Royal Society of Literature's Encore Award, and listed among the Best Novels of 2022 by *Grazia*, *Glamour*, and *The Irish Times*. Driven by her own experience of rape, Winnie founded Clear Lines, the UK's first festival addressing sexual assault and consent through the arts, and began her PhD research at the London School of Economics. Winnie has given over 200 public talks and appeared on the BBC, Sky News, Channel 4, *The Guardian*, and TEDx London. She holds an honorary doctorate from the National University of Ireland in recognition of her work.

Wenyan Lu is a native of Shanghai who moved to the UK in 2006. Wenyan holds a Master of Studies in Creative Writing from the University of Cambridge. Her historical novel *The Martyr's Hymn* was longlisted for The SI Leeds Literary Prize in 2018 and Bridport First Novel Prize in 2019. Her novel *The Funeral Cryer* won The SI Leeds Literary Prize in 2020. *The Funeral Cryer* was published in hardback and ebook by Allen and Unwin in the UK in May, 2022 and July in Australia and New Zealand. The audio version was released in June, 2023 by W.F. Howes. The book will also be published in the US and Canada by HarperCollins and in Italy by Garzanti in Spring, 2024. The UK paperback edition will be launched in April, 2024. Wenyan Lives in Cambridge with her husband Mark and two children, Sean and Carys.

Amita Murray's novel *Unladylike Lessons in Love* explores colonial history and its place in our stories, lives and imaginations. Her Regency novels are published with HarperCollins. Her novel *Thirteenth Night* won the Exeter Novel Prize and her collection *Marmite and Mango Chutney* won the SI Leeds Literary Prize in 2016. Her most recent short story came out in *Ellery Queen Mystery Magazine*, one of the largest mystery magazines in the world. She has been writer in residence with the British Council, Spread the Word, Literature Works and Leverhulme.

Irenosen Okojie is a Nigerian British author whose work pushes the boundaries of form, language, and ideas. Her novel

Butterfly Fish, and short story collections, *Speak Gigantular* and *Nudibranch*, have won and been nominated for multiple awards. Her journalism has been featured in *The New York Times*, *The Observer*, *The Guardian* and *The Huffington Post*. She is a Contributing Editor for *The White Review*. She co-presented the BBC's 'Turn Up For The Books' podcast alongside Simon Savidge and Bastille frontman, Dan Smith. Her work has been optioned for the screen. She has also judged various literary prizes including the Dylan Thomas Prize, The Gordon Burn Prize as well as the BBC National Short Story Award. She was a judge for the 2023 Women's Prize For Fiction. Vice Chair of the Royal Society of Literature, she was awarded an MBE For Services to Literature in 2021. She is the director and founder of Black to the Future festival.

Yoanna Pak is a London based Canadian. She moved to London after working retail in Paris, France and teaching secondary school in Seoul, South Korea. Her writing career began when she applied to the MA in Creative Writing programme at Goldsmiths College to avoid deportation back to Canada. 'Wolnam', her first novel, was born at Goldsmiths. Its beginning chapters were shortlisted for the Pat Kavanagh Prize, and it has been shortlisted for the SI Leeds Literary Prize and longlisted for the Virginia Prize for Fiction. A husband and two children later, she hopes to publish 'Wolnam' and finally finish her PhD.

Huma Qureshi is an award-winning writer, author of the novel, *Playing Games*, the memoir *How We Met*, shortlisted for the Indie Book Awards, and the short story collection *Things We Do Not Tell The People We Love*, longlisted for the Jhalak Prize and the Edge Hill Prize, both published in 2021. She lives in London.

Minoli Salgado is a novelist, memoirist and world-leading postcolonial scholar with expertise in migrant and Sri Lankan literary studies. She is the author of the critical monograph, *Writing Sri Lanka: Literature, Resistance and the Politics of Place* (2007); the novel, *A Little Dust on the Eyes* (2014), winner of the first SI Leeds Literary Prize; a collection of short stories, *Broken Jaw* (2019), shortlisted for the Republic of Consciousness Prize and longlisted for the Orwell Prize for Political Fiction; and a book of narrative non-fiction, *Twelve Cries from Home: In Search of Sri Lanka's Disappeared* (2022), based on victim-survivor narratives from the Sri Lankan civil war. Her Leverhulme-funded study on transnational witness literature is forthcoming with Bloomsbury Academic. She is currently Professor of International Writing at Manchester Metropolitan University.

Valerie Saunders graduated in English Literature from the University of Nottingham a long time ago, and spent her professional life working well away from the arts, for the most part managing services in the NHS. She is not a writer! Through her membership of Soroptimist International of Leeds she had the opportunity to be involved in setting up the club's new literary prize for unpublished fiction a decade or more ago. Val has been closely involved ever since, first as the Chair of the Prize Steering Group, and now chairing its Advisory Group. Through its years of development, the Prize has given her the opportunity and privilege both to nurture her own love of reading and to celebrate the discovery of new authors.

Yvonne Singh is a journalist, editor and writer. Her work has been published in *The Guardian*, *The Observer*, *The White Review*, *BBC History*, *The Mirror* and *The London Evening Standard*, among others. She lectures in narrative non-fiction, fiction and journalism at London's City Lit. Her short stories have been shortlisted for the Seán Ó Faoláin prize, Black Spring Press prize and longlisted for the Brick Lane Bookshop Prize. She was a contributor to *Know Your Place*, an anthology of working-class writing (her essay inspired an exhibition *Seaside: Photographed*, which toured UK galleries) and in 2018, she was second runner-up for the SI Leeds Literary Prize. She is currently working on a narrative non-fiction book about the history of the Black and minority ethnic press in the UK.

Mahsuda Snaith is a writer of novels and short stories. After the release of her debut novel *The Things We Thought We Knew* she was named an 'Observer New Face of Fiction'. Her second novel *How to Find Home* was broadcast on BBC Radio 4. She is the winner of the SI Leeds Literary Prize 2014 and Bristol Short Story Prize 2014. Mahsuda has led creative writing workshops in universities, hospitals, schools and a homeless hostel and has worked as a writing mentor for a variety of writing organisations. She is a commissioned writer for the 'Colonial Countryside' project and her short story 'The Panther's Tale' is included in *Hag: Forgotten Folktales Retold*. Mahsuda works as a writing coach at The Novelry. Find out more about her work at www.mahsudasnaith.com

Shereen Tadros is apparently better at writing fiction than she is at writing her author bio. She has won various awards, including from the National Centre for Writing and Arts Council England. When not writing, she works as a doctor in a children's hospital and looks after her four children. Both these pursuits involve more encounters with clowns than she is comfortable with. Her manuscript, 'Say Goodbye to Her', was the winner of the 2018 SI Leeds Literary Prize.

ROLL OF HONOUR

2012 Prize

Longlist:
A Little Dust on the Eyes – Minoli Salgado
A Tiny Speck of Black and Then Nothing – Emily Midorikawa
Beneath the Fretting Rainbow – Sylvia Dickinson
Borrowed Light – Karen Onojaife
Broken Jaw – Minoli Salgado
Seduce – Désirée Reynolds
Storybank: The Milkfarm Years – Jane Steele
The Book of Ghosts – Katy Massey
The Clouds Floated By – Donna Edinboro
The March of Aida – Emma Allotey
The Secret Arts – Azma Dar
The Weekend for Sex & Other Stories – Anita Sivakumaran

Shortlist:
A Little Dust on the Eyes – Minoli Salgado
A Tiny Speck of Black and Then Nothing – Emily Midorikawa
Borrowed Light – Karen Onojaife
Storybank: The Milkfarm Years – Jane Steele
The Book of Ghosts – Katy Massey
The Weekend for Sex & Other Stories – Anita Sivakumaran

Winners:
1. A Little Dust on the Eyes – Minoli Salgado
2. Borrowed Light – Karen Onojaife
3. Jointly: Storybank: The Milkfarm Years – Jane Steele
and A Tiny Speck of Black and Then Nothing – Emily Midorikawa

SI Readers' Choice: Borrowed Light – Karen Onojaife

2014 Prize

Longlist:
Red Is for Later and Other Stories – Farah Ahamed
Bloody's in the Bible – Muli Amaye
Hanging from the Hammer of the Bell – Season Butler
Those Who Understand – Azma Dar
Stories My Mother Told Me – Katy Massey
The Khan – Saima Mir
The Spaces Between Us – Emma Norry
A Mouthful of Silence – Reshma Ruia
The Queen – Anita Sivakumaran
The Constellation of Ravine Roy – Mahsuda Snaith
Secrets of the Land – Atuki Turner
Blue in Green – Kit De Waal

Shortlist:
Red Is for Later and Other Stories – Farah Ahamed
Hanging from the Hammer of the Bell – Season Butler
A Mouthful of Silence – Reshma Ruia
The Queen – Anita Sivakumaran
The Constellation of Ravine Roy – Mahsuda Snaith
Blue in Green – Kit De Waal

Winners:
1. The Constellation of Ravine Roy – Mahsuda Snaith
2. Hanging from the Hammer of the Bell – Season Butler
3. The Queen – Anita Sivakumaran

SI Readers' Choice: Blue in Green – Kit de Waal

2016 Prize

Longlist:
Recognising Strangers – Jamilah Ahmed
Deadly Sacrifice – Stella Akinade-Ahmadou
When Skies Are Grey – Fran Clark
The Ice Migration – Jacqueline Crooks
Our Staggering Minds – Harkiran Dhindsa
Truth – Roshi Fernando
Runaway – Divya Ghelani
Dark Chapter – Winnie M Li
Marmite and Mango Chutney – Amita Murray
Waking Hours – Anushka Rasiah
Coloured In – Yazmin Raven
Scent of a Feather – Fariyal Wallez

Shortlist:
Recognising Strangers – Jamilah Ahmed
Deadly Sacrifice – Stella Akinade-Ahmadou
When Skies Are Grey – Fran Clark
Our Staggering Minds – Harkiran Dhindsa
Dark Chapter – Winnie M Li
Marmite and Mango Chutney – Amita Murray

Winners:
1. Amita Murray – Marmite and Mango Chutney
2. Winnie M Li – Dark Chapter
3. Jamilah Ahmed – Recognising Strangers

SI Readers' Choice: Jamilah Ahmed – Recognising Strangers

2018 Prize

Longlist:
Baba Ji on Boulton Road – Kavita Bhanot
A Scattering of Blue Moons – Lynne E Blackwood
Sisterhood of Swans – Selma Carvalho
Let Us Look Elsewhere – Mona Dash
Hibiscus, Rose, Jacaranda – Omega Douglas
Lying Perfectly Still – Laura Fish
Manual for a Decent Life – Kavita A Jindal
The Hymn of Lei Feng – Wenyan Lu
Wolnam – Yoanna Pak
Kololo Hill – Neema Shah
One Man's Revolution – Yvonne Singh
Say Goodbye to Her – Shereen Tadros

Shortlist:
Baba Ji on Boulton Road – Kavita Bhanot
Let Us Look Elsewhere – Mona Dash
Hibiscus, Rose, Jacaranda – Omega Douglas
Wolnam – Yoanna Pak
One Man's Revolution – Yvonne Singh
Say Goodbye To Her – Shereen Tadros

Winners:
1. Say Goodbye To Her – Shereen Tadros
2. One Man's Revolution – Yvonne Singh
3. Baba Ji on Boulton Road – Kavita Bhanot

SI Readers' Choice: Hibiscus, Rose, Jacaranda – Omega Douglas

2020 Prize

Judges: Niki Chang (chair), Malika Booker, Kadija George, Yvonne Singh

Longlist:
The Funeral Cryer – Wenyan Lu
The Sun Sets in the East – L M Dillsworth
The Good Twin – Sumana Khan
A Boy called Silence – Nana Afua A Pierre
Bat Monkey and Other Stories – Aisha Phoenix
Her Grandmother's Ghost – Ulka Karandikar
In the Skin of a Stranger – Alinah Azadeh
Lying Perfectly Still – Laura Fish
Mushrooms for my Mother and Other Stories – Ethel Maqeda
Nothing Stays in the Dark Forever – Steffanie Edward
The Change – Emma Hill
Things We Do Not Tell the People We Love – Huma Qureshi
Unborn – Tanya Atapattu

Shortlist:
The Funeral Cryer – Wenyan Lu
The Sun Sets in the East – L M Dillsworth
The Good Twin – Sumana Khan
A Boy called Silence – Nana Afua A Pierre
Bat Monkey and Other Stories – Aisha Phoenix
Things We Do Not Tell the People We Love – Huma Qureshi

Winners:
1. The Funeral Cryer – Wenyan Lu
2. The Sun Sets in the East – L M Dillsworth
3. The Good Twin – Sumana Khan

SI Readers' Choice: The Good Twin – Sumana Khan

2022 Prize

Longlist:
Lying Perfectly Still – Laura Fish
Night School – Divya Ghelani
The Taste of a Planet – Arianne Maki
Kala Polari – Clare Ramsaran
Sometimes the Sky is Blue – Latoyah Innerarity
Scattering Stars Like Dust – Mona Dash
To Have Not, To Hold – Monica Clarke
Aralola Will Be Absolutely Fine – Oluwaseun Oluwatosin Akinsiku
All the Truths Between Us – Liz Amos
Never Enough – Suad Kamardeen
Invincible Jacarandas – Zahirra Dayal
When You're Smiling – Nazira Vania

Shortlist
Lying Perfectly Still - Laura Fish
The Taste of a Planet - Arianne Maki
Sometimes the Sky is Blue - Latoyah Innerarity
Aralola Will Be Absolutely Fine - Oluwaseun Oluwatosin Akinsiku
Never Enough - Suad Kamardeen
When You're Smiling - Nazira Vania

Winners:
1. Never Enough – Suad Kamardeen
2. Sometimes the Sky is Blue – Latoyah Innerarity
3. Lying Perfectly Still – Laura Fish

SI Readers' Choice: Lying Perfectly Still – Laura Fish

ACKNOWLEDGEMENTS

SI Literary Prize is grateful for the continued support of its core partners and funders:

In addition, the prize receives support from a range of other excellent partners, including Arvon, Mslexia, New Writing North, The Literary Consultancy and The Opportunity Centre. Together, these partnerships have enabled the prize to flourish, and we simply could not continue without them – thank you.